Television Production
for
Education

TV Production for Education

A Systems Approach

Peter Combes & John Tiffin

Focal Press · London

Focal/Hastings House · New York

First Edition 1978

British Library Cataloguing in Publication Data

Combes, Peter
    Television production for education
    1. Television — Production and direction
    2. Television in education
    I. Title   II. Tiffin, John
    791'45'5   LB1044.8   77–30386

    ISBN (excl. USA) 0 240 50952 8
    ISBN (USA only) 0 8038 7178 3

Printed in Great Britain
by Thomson Litho Ltd, East Kilbride, Scotland

Contents

PN
1992.75
.C65

5

size information; Lack of third dimension; Contradiction or distraction; Duplication; Cueing; Setting; The limitations – a mnemonic; Resource limitations.

third source; Separate clearing of cameras; Walk in shot; Editing; Advanced techniques.

Preface

Television production is a complex process.

The idea of taking a systems approach to the process is an original and very sensible one, especially at a time when new developments in technology (lightweight video cameras, digitally controlled editing, etc.) are leading to a further expansion in the use of television in education. One of the results of these developments is an increase in the numbers of those taking responsibility for production without any previous training.

This book will be of great value to teachers or others faced with the problem of how to make the most effective use of television equipment. Although the authors describe an approach to the subject that will be useful to those in the most advanced educational television systems, the principles of it can be applied in much less sophisticated situations at home or abroad.

If there is one aspect of the text to which great attention should be given, it is the section within part II entitled "The Production System". The education television producer ignores at his or her peril the authors' advice about educationalists, which are crucial to successful production processes, and therefore to the rest of the book.

For example, the Open University's solution to this problem has been the development of a 'course team'. This is a group of people responsible to the relevant Faculty of the Open University for the production of all course materials, that is, printed correspondence texts, television and radio broadcasts. The team is composed of academics, educational technologists (concerned about pre-testing of material as well as full-scale research – see 'The Evaluation

System') and television and radio producers. In this way the role of the producer is seen not as ancillary, but central to the educational purposes of the institution he or she serves.

This book should serve to help the beginner and will also perhaps remind the more experienced producer of the crucial value of taking a systematic approach to production, and that much more than 'recording educational material' is involved. If it is successful, the authors will have helped producers considerably towards achieving the most desired of 'outputs', Miltons "plainest taught and easiest learnt".

The authors, graduates of the Universities of Cambridge and Leeds in Mathematics and Geography respectively, combine an unusual range of experience in the comparatively new profession of educational television. In the last decade they have worked separately in a number of developing countries in Africa and North and South America, and have together published a number of studies concerning problems of teaching by television. Whether working in Britain or for the Centre for Educational Television Overseas (later Broadcasting Division, Centre for Educational Development Overseas and now part of the British Council) or overseas, they have had particular responsibilities for the training of educational television producers and have been preparing this book as a result of their joint experience, over a considerable time. In 1976 John Tiffin was awarded a doctorate in educational technology by Florida State University, one of the leading institutions in this field.

1 Introduction

Systems within systems

In the first few pages of this book we explain what is meant by a systems approach and how you can use such an approach to plan, prepare and produce television for education.

To understand the value of a systems approach, try this test before going any further:

'Write, as best you can, a script for a three-minute instructional television programme about your home town.'

When you are ready, read on.

*   *   *

Did you write a script?
Does your script begin with credits?
Is there music with the credits?
Do you have a presenter?
Are the presenter's first remarks something like, 'Hello, children, welcome to today's programme on. ....'?

If you did any of these things you were probably not using a systems approach. You were copying a popular idea of what an instructional television programme should be like.

If you did *not* write a script – if, instead, you asked, 'What is the purpose of the programme? Who is it for? How will it be used?' – then you were applying a systems approach.

A systems approach means that you begin the process of production by finding the answer to the question 'What is the objective of the programme(s) I am asked to produce?' Having got a clear answer, you go about production so as to achieve these objectives.

This sounds very simple and logical, and indeed it is. However, very little educational television is produced in this way. Most producers are asked to make a programme *about* something. They are told what the content of the programme should be, instead its purpose in terms of the audience. This is not merely a matter of semantics. It leads to a different way of looking at things and a different way of producing television.

First, you need to know some of the basic concepts of systems thinking. A system is a set of interrelated parts which function together to cause change. What goes into a system to make changes is called *input*. The function of change in a system is called *process*. The outcome of the changes a system makes is referred to as *output*.

The relationships can be shown by a diagram. These symbols are widely used:

A television camera is a system. One of its inputs is a set of light rays. The camera *processes* the light rays and the *output* is a set of electrical impulses (the video signal).

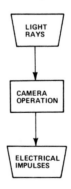

A studio monitor is a system. Its input is electrical impulses. The monitor processes the impulses and the resulting output is a picture.

A television director is a system. One of his inputs is the picture from a monitor. The director analyzes the picture (process), and makes a decision as to whether to change the picture or to accept it (for recording or transmission). In this case there are two possible outputs and the decision point is shown on the diagram by a diamond. A decision 'yes' is shown by the sign '+' and a decision 'no' is shown by the sign '−'.

12

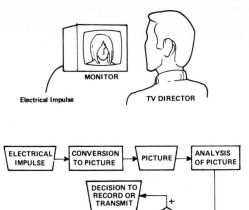

The studio monitor and the director himself as *systems*.

Systems within systems

A television director is a *living system*. The camera and the monitor are *machine systems*. Living systems and machine systems can function together as *man-machine systems*. A television camera and its operator form a man-machine system. A television studio is also a man-machine system. There is, however, a difference in degree between a camera-operator system and a television studio system. The camera-operator system is interacting with other camera-operator systems, with microphone systems, illumination systems, actors, the director, and so on, all operating as parts of the studio system. It is the interaction of these *subsystems* which enables the studio system to televise a television programme.

A television studio or any kind of outside broadcast unit is a *televising system*. A televising system interacts with planning and preparing systems as parts of the *suprasystem* of production. An instructional television production system is part of an instructional television suprasystem, which in turn is part of an educational suprasystem.

The terms suprasystem and subsystem are relative. A particular system may be a subsystem of one system and the suprasystem of another. For example, to an optician, a lens is a system and a camera a suprasystem. To a cameraman, a camera is a system, and a studio is a suprasystem. To a director, a studio is a system, a camera is a subsystem, and the instructional television system is a suprasystem. *What is important is the concept of systems within systems.*

13

Although your primary concern is with the production system and its three basic subsystems (planning, preparation and televising), you must refer to the instructional television system as a whole. This is the suprasystem that the production system serves.

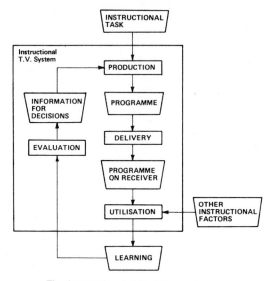

The instructional television system.

2 Instructional television system

An instructional television system has four sub-systems: production, delivery, utilisation and evaluation.

Delivery system

This is the system which brings the television programme to the learner. Its output is the sound and image on a television receiver or monitor in a place where the learners can watch and listen. It can take many forms:

TV. STATION   HOMES   SCHOOLS   COMMUNITY CENTRES

1. OPEN TRANSMISSION SYSTEM

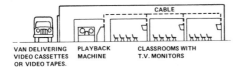

CABLE

VAN DELIVERING   PLAYBACK   CLASSROOMS WITH
VIDEO CASSETTES   MACHINE   T.V. MONITORS
OR VIDEO TAPES.

2. CLOSED CIRCUIT SYSTEM

Types of delivery system.

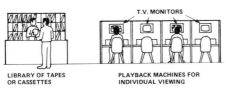

T.V. MONITORS

LIBRARY OF TAPES   PLAYBACK MACHINES FOR
OR CASSETTES   INDIVIDUAL VIEWING

3. LIBRARY SYSTEM

15

Evaluation system

One instructional television system produced a regular schedule of programmes for two years before discovering that none of the schools for which the programmes were intended was watching them.

If the output of a system is not satisfactory, it can be changed, provided that the system receives information about its ouput. This is known as *feedback*.

To function efficiently, a system needs to measure its inputs, its outputs, and its internal processes in such a way that decisions can be made to effect change for the better. Such meaningful measurement is called *Evaluation*.

Your aim as a producer is not simply to produce programmes but to produce programmes which achieve specified instructional objectives. You must know to what extent your programmes promote learning so that you can decide whether to remake the programmes for future use.

Utilisation system

The output of this system is learning, which is also the output of the instructional television system as a whole.

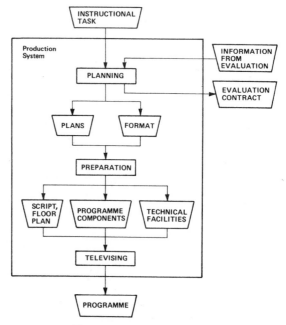

The production system.

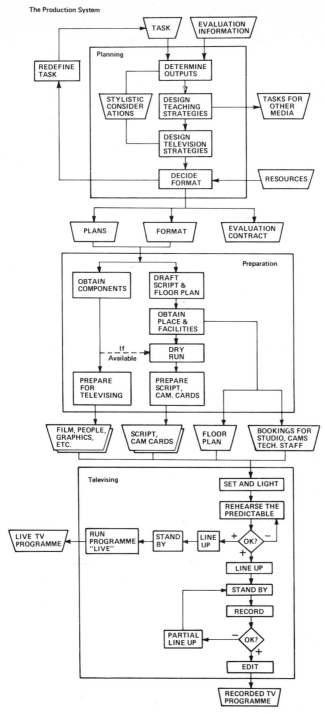

The Production System

The production system: planning, preparation and televising.

The process of this system consists of organizing a situation so that learning can take place as a result of watching and listening to a television programme. The situation may be organized by teachers or by the learners themselves.

Nobody knows exactly how learning takes place. Just looking at television may not ensure learning. Often other inputs besides the television programme need to be involved. For example, learning may take place through the influence of a teacher, a text, or other factors in conjunction with television.

The diagram on page 16 is in a simplified form. The complete system is shown on page 17.

Production system

In the rest of this book we describe the production system. There are three sections, which correspond to the subsystems – planning, preparing and televising.

In each section each process that concerns the producer is examined in detail. When you are working with each subsystem try to keep the whole system (or suprasystem) in mind.

This key diagram will help you to know where you are, at each stage:

3 Planning system – I

The amount of time, thought and detail involved in planning programmes with many educational objectives for an audience of millions is greater than is required for a simple programme for a small audience. The basic processes, however, are the same. They are shown in the following diagram.

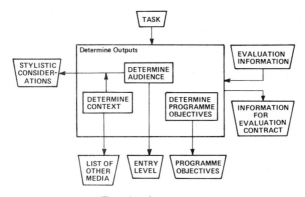

The planning system.

From page 21 onwards, there are sections that examine each of these processes in detail. First, a note on the people involved in planning.

In order to plan television for teaching, someone must know how to teach, someone must know what to teach, and someone must be able to translate the 'what' and 'how' into television.

If you can do all these three things you are a rare person. It is more likely that you will be working with a teacher. If the instructional task is difficult or the content is complicated, you will need a teaching specialist or a subject matter specialist.

People from the world of education and those from the world of television do not mix easily. In many instructional television systems the work of production is rigidly compartmentalised. The educationalists plan the programmes and write the scripts. The television producer 'visualises' the script.

Avoid such a situation. It produces neither good education nor good television. Work with the educationalists *as a team* through each stage of planning. You will also need to consult with them at other stages in production.

Teachers often have fixed ideas about teaching, and television producers develop strong ideas about the programme they would like to do. The team should be conscious of these tendencies and try to be flexible and open to new ideas.

Determine the outputs

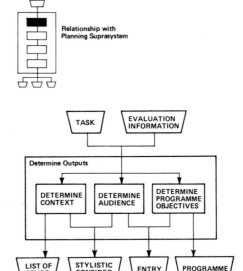

Determine outputs. Note the relationship with the suprasystem, here and in other diagrams.

You need to know, in clear, measurable terms:
who (the target audience) will learn what (the educational objectives) where (the educational system, other media in use, conditions of reception).

20

You need the following information:

Audience

Entry level
Age range
Socio-economic factors
Educational level
Linguistic factors
Motivation

Context of Use

Reception – open or closed
Physical context
Media context

Evaluation Information

Results of previous programmes

Objectives

Programme objectives – as given

Audience

What is the *entry level* of the audience? In other words, what will you
assume that the audience already knows? Your programme is a 'vehicle' to take the learners from where they are to where they want to be.
What you are doing at this stage is determining the starting point. In a
controlled instructional system such as a school or a university, the
starting point is usually predetermined. A programme for third year
medical students will have the first two years of medicine as a prerequisite.

Imagine, however, that you are given the following task:

*A community development project in a rural area is based on new
techniques of farming, which will be taught by television. The rural
communities do not yet have television receivers, but sets will be supplied.*

*Produce a programme with the object of teaching the target
audience how to adjust their receivers.*

How much does the audience already know about adjusting
receivers? Do they know enough to switch on a receiver and obtain

21

some sort of picture, or do they know nothing at all about television? In the first case, you could make a programme which would explain (via the audio channel) how to adjust the set so that the audience obtains a good quality picture. In the second case, a technician or some other qualified person would be needed to switch on the receiver and adjust the set.

The programme would then explain how to operate the receiver and would demonstrate common errors.

A series of programmes to teach reading and writing skills to children may have the same entry level as a series to teach the same skills to adults. However, the styles of the two programmes should be very different. Your choice of words, pictures, music, and, perhaps, even content, will depend on the characteristics of the audience. You need information about the vocabulary and language style of your audience, their intellectual capacity and their 'conceptual frame of reference'.

Here is an example of a 'conceptual frame of reference' problem:
Look at this photograph (opposite).

Is the water part of a lake? a fresh water river? an estuary? What does the picture tell *you*?

Your answers will depend on *your* conceptual frame of reference. This picture was shown to a fisherman in Brazil who said, 'A fishing port. What big tides they have! They fish for lobster. What kind of boat do they keep in that shed?' Would you have recognised the visual features which gave him this information?

Find out how old your learners are. Are they rich or poor? Urban or rural? White collar or blue collar? What kind of education have they had? What language or dialect do they speak. They are basic guides to the character of the audience. The nature of a particular programme may mean that you need further information. As you study these factors, you will find a concept of your audience developing.

Keep referring to this throughout the production process. Some producers try to keep in mind a person who they think epitomises the audience.

What does the audience hope to gain from the programme? What is their *motivation* for attending a reception centre or switching on their set to watch an instructional programme? It may be that the target audience has no alternative — school children may watch because their teacher wishes them to see the programme. In that case, why does *the teacher* want to use the programme in his classes? The producer needs to know this because if the programmes do not provide what the teacher wants, the teacher will stop using them. Adult audiences who wish to learn something are strongly self-motivated, but if they feel *they* are not getting what they want from a programme they will be quick to switch off. You must know what motivates your audience.

When audiences are heterogeneous, the problem of audience analysis can be severe. Imagine the problems attached to producing the programme on how to adjust a television receiver if the rural population in question were that of a country such as India. The enormous size of the audience and the critical importance of the programme (the whole project collapses if no one can adjust the television receiver) warrant the expenditure of much time and energy on audience analysis.

When audiences are relatively homogeneous, audience analysis can be simple.

For example, in a typical closed-circuit schools television service, the producer may simply need to know the grade for which he is producing. (He then knows the age range and educational level, the language and the dialect that the children speak. The curriculum is

Here is an example of a 'conceptual frame of reference' problem: Look at this photograph.
Is the water part of a lake, a fresh water river, or an estuary? What does the picture tell *you*? Your answers will depend on *your* conceptual frame of reference.

based on what the audience knows and a meeting with the teachers involved will make it clear what they want from the television programmes).

Schools have detailed records of their students and departments of education function on the basis of statistical information about the educational system they control. States relate planned development to statistics about their population.

There are census departments and foundations concerned with obtaining population statistics for planning and assessing economic development.

Audience research organisations conduct surveys to determine specific information about broadcasting expressly for the benefit for broadcasters.

Manuals of yearly statistics are published for many fields.

In a closed circuit system with a relatively homogeneous audience you can obtain valuable information (data) about each person in your audience.

Show this data on bar graphs.

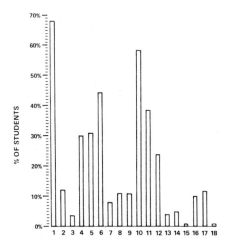

Bar graph to show entry level of knowledge of students for each of 18 instructional objectives.

Now you can see the characteristics of the majority of your audience. In any large audience there will be some individuals at the extremes of the curve: there is a danger that by trying to reach the extremes you will generalise your programme so that it loses its impact. Television is a mass medium. Leave the extremes to other media. By teaching the majority, television can liberate teachers to concentrate on the special cases.

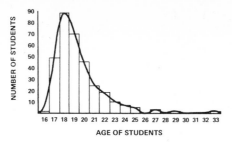

AGE OF STUDENTS

Frequency curve to show age distribution of students taking a university course. The mid-points of the tops of the pillars are connected by a curving line, to make group data clear.

If your frequency curve shows two or more well separated 'peaks' you have two different types of learner. You should be thinking of two separate programmes or of a series.

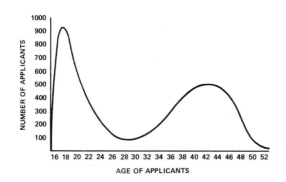

AGE OF APPLICANTS

Frequency curve to show ages of applicants for a teacher-training course.

Above is a 'frequency curve' with two peaks. The first peak consists of young people, most of whom are unmarried and fresh out of school. The second peak consists mainly of married women whose children are going to school, permitting them to take up a professional career.

One group has first hand knowledge of current schooling, but little first hand knowledge of children. The other group has first hand knowledge of children but a concept of school as it was twenty or more years before.

The techniques for tabulating and describing data about everyone in your audience belongs to *descriptive statistics*. You could master the skills involved from a basic handbook or course on statistics.

If you are trying to determine the main characteristics of a very large heterogeneous audience in places where you employ open transmission you may need to use *inferential statistics*. The techniques of inferential statistics enable you to make inferences about the characteristics of the audience as a whole from an analysis of a sample of the population.

If you need to sample your audience call in a person or organisation with skill in handling statistics – the techniques involved are complex and sophisticated.

Get a feel for what the statistics mean. Go and meet your audience. Go into the classrooms, the playgrounds, the common rooms, wherever you sit and talk to the people who will use and learn from your programmes.

The trick is to listen rather than talk. Let them tell you rather than your telling them.

Context of use

When an audience can decide how much television it will watch, and how frequently, we can say there is *open reception*. In this situation the audience and the utilisation of programmes is not controlled. Many television stations broadcast language programmes for open reception. Some schools broadcasting systems fall into this category. The teachers study a television timetable and then decide whether to use a particular series or a particular programme. When there is open reception, your audience is likely to be heterogeneous; also you cannot be sure that the audience for one programme is the same as the one that watched the previous programme or will watch the next. Each programme must be self-sufficient. Each programme must attract its audience and implant an incentive to watch the next.

Closed reception is when the audience and the utilisation of programmes is controlled. A course may be organised, for example by closed-circuit system, so that the content is presented by television. To attend the course, the student must use television. In 'television schools' children attend in order to receive instruction by the medium of television.

In closed reception you can 'tailor' your programmes precisely. You know the same people watch each time, so your programmes can depend on each other. You will have a relatively homogeneous audience, so you can make your messages more direct. Reception is controlled and organised to eliminate distractions. You are not competing for the attention of the audience.

Will your audience be watching at home? In this case there are usually a lot of distractions, including, perhaps, competition from other members of the family who want to watch a programme on another channel. The student needs a lot of self-discipline. This kind of reception is viable for the intelligent, highly motivated learner, and with a very attractive format it is even possible to compete with commercial programmes for the attention of children and effectively teach them. Remember that the situation has a lot of distractions. Do not plan instructional sequences which demand concentrated attention for long periods. Introduce a relaxing 'break' or a change of subject before you lose the attention of the least well motivated in your audience – or keep the programme short. Repeat important ideas during the programme.

Repeat the programme at least once, and repeat the ideas again in the next programme.

Can your audience be organised to watch together in groups? Some people find trying to view instructional programmes alone is not as easy or as pleasant as in a group. Moreover, a group of people can help each other to learn. There are two ways in which this happens. One is called 'Peer Teaching'. This simply means that two learners help each other to learn. If one person has not understood a part of the programme, then it is possible that the other person can help. Peer teaching is surprisingly effective and needs very little organisation. The other method is to use 'Group Dynamics'. After an educational programme, a group of between three and eight people interact with each other by discussion, debate, or exercises to achieve the instructional objectives of the programme together. (Groups of more than eight are unwieldy and begin to break up into subgroups). You need to know how the interaction functions so that your programme can 'feed' the group activities.

With group reception situations repetition is not so important, nor need you always be considering the least able persons in your audience.

The group will do much of the reinforcing involved in repetition and will help the slower learner or those who missed a programme, or part of it.

Is your audience in a school or similar centre where reception is in organised groups? In this case a 'monitor' or teacher will be in charge of reception and utilisation. The learners will be organised for a sequence of learning activities of which the television programme is one. Find out what is intended to be the role of television. Design your programme to relate directly to the other instructional processes. This sounds obvious, but television programmes made for schools are often designed as a 'set piece', as though the purpose of the lesson were to watch the television programme. Programmes of this nature ignore the teacher and finish with a long string of credits and a theatrical flourish of closing music. Watch the effect this kind of ending has on a class. Students become restless; they feel that the show is over. An inexperienced teacher may have to struggle for control. The experienced teacher switches the receiver off before the end title sequence begins. What then was the function of the complicated ending? Compare this with the ending, 'You have seen examples of the large scale use of iron and steel. How many small scale examples of its use can you see in your classroom?'

The programme now ends, beginning an exercise, and signalling to the classroom teacher to take over.

Will the audience view the programme in a library? In some educational institutions television can be viewed by the learner in a library where he can request a programme and watch it by himself in a cubicle or 'carrel'. Such a student does not have to face the distractions of domestic viewing, and can view a programme or part of it more than once. It may be possible to stop the tape at any time, in some cases even holding a single-frame image.

Media content

Television is sometimes used by itself to achieve an educational aim. A children's programme intended to give an idea of what it is like to live in a different country may be transmitted in 'entertainment time' and all the information that is considered necessary is contained in the programme. Similarly, a news programme or an outside broadcast of an important event may be transmitted without any other medium being used.

Television can have strong emotional impact if used in this way, and can also achieve immediate results that are impossible with other media. Its very wide range of distribution, even for areas with severe communication difficulties, may also have been a reason for deciding to use television.

However, any medium has its own limitations. A pupil reading a book may stop at any point he does not understand and go back to read again the part he found difficult the first time. He may be able to look up the difficult point in another book, or even, in some cases, leave the problem for a while and come back to it later. If using a videotape or videocassette machine he may be able to do something similar, but with other kinds of television the pupil must be able to keep up with the rhythm and speed of the programme or he is lost. He cannot control or even influence the speed of the presentation and he cannot ask questions. For reference purposes, television is even more limited – there is, as yet, no television equivalent to the dictionary or the encyclopaedia, in which things can be 'looked up' as required. To teach people how to operate a machine, the television receiver can show, sometimes with greater facility than even a 'live' demonstration, what actions need to be carried out. But, it cannot, in itself, provide the learners with actual practice in doing them.

The above are some of the reasons why it is often necessary to use television in combination with other media. A television course in touch-typing would require that each pupil had a suitable typewriter, or at least some kind of a model with appropriate realism. A series on chemical reactions could well be supplemented by a large poster of the periodic table which could be kept in the classroom for reference, a geography programme by a large scale map of the region being described, an art series by high definition colour reproductions of standard works, and so on. In language work, the real-life situations shown in the programmes could be linked with dictionaries for reference and audio cassettes for practice.

In these examples, the important 'core teaching' is done by television, but it is also possible for television material to supplement core teaching by another medium. Even the language teaching example given above is a borderline case – the core grammatical work might be given by a teacher, with the dictionaries, audio cassettes and television supplementing his or her work.

A correspondence course on social studies might be supplemented by television programmes containing interviews and discussions. A book on the political history of the twentieth century might contain videodiscs of scenes from the periods involved. In these examples the television material supplements the core teaching given by another medium.

It is essential that you know what role your television programme is to fulfil in the overall teaching strategy. Is yours the responsibility for the 'core teaching'? Do you have to decide what other media are to be used? If your programmes is to supplement core teaching by another medium, what precisely is the role of television?

Be particularly careful that if a classroom teacher is to be involved, his role be clearly defined and understood by all concerned. Educational television can actually come to grief in this way. A classroom teacher, well qualified and experienced, may be jealous, and understandably, of any attempt to encroach on his prerogatives as the one responsible for the teaching given, though he may accept the 'help' of television in doing something that is obviously impossible for the classroom teacher. A music teacher might welcome the opportunity for his class to see and hear a professional presentation of a symphony, while he will be annoyed, even to the point of switching the receiver off, if the television teacher starts to explain key notation. At the other end of the scale, in a system designed so that 'core teaching' is given by the television set for the benefit of a class supervised by an unqualified monitor, the latter may complain that he is being put in an impossible position if the television programme does *not* do all the vital teaching. *It is thus of critical importance that the intended role of the classroom teacher, if any, is understood equally by you and by the teacher(s).*

Obviously the combination of media being used has a greater chance of success if each medium is occupied with tasks that are within its capabilities and use the opportunities offered. Television is at its best when exploiting its ability to give widely varying experiences beyond the physical reach of the viewer, perhaps by drama, or by showing scenes from distant places, or offering contact with people who could not visit the viewer or, again, by showing things that would be too expensive or too difficult to show by other means. In contrast, the impossibility of having the viewer 'pace' the presentation, the low definition, and the ephemeral nature of the programme makes it less suitable for some kinds of work than other media. If you can participate in the allocation of tasks to the various media, do not hesitate to transfer to other available media the tasks that they can do better. This will enable you to concentrate on the tasks that television can do well.

Evaluation information

Has the programme been made before? If so – what was the evaluation? In instructional television, programmes are often remade for no apparent reason. Does the recording still exist? Don't remake it unless you can improve it. Which parts of the previous programme were unsatisfactory? Why?

Instructional objectives

You may be given carefully prepared and very specific objectives. You must be able to understand these. You are like a builder receiving carefully drawn blueprints which show exactly what has to be built.

On the other hand, you may have to work with someone who gives you vague objectives. It is as though a builder is approached by someone without plans who simply asks him to build a house. The builder cannot work from this. He must ask, 'How big a house?' 'How many rooms?' 'What size rooms?' 'What shape of house?' In fact, to do the work, the builder must somehow translate what the man has in mind into a working blueprint. In the same way, if you are given a vague objective you must somehow elicit a precise description from which to work.

30

Unfortunately, instructional objectives have become a complicated issue with a confusing array of terms, many of which have overlapping meanings. What follows is a brief guide to the different kinds of objectives you may meet:

Content objectives

Teach map reading to the eighth grade.
Show rural communities how to adjust a television receiver.
Explain the importance of group dynamics to trainee teachers.

The operative verb is usually 'teach', but it could also be 'explain', 'demonstrate', or 'show'. It describes what the teacher does and implies some form of presentation or exposition of the subject. The object of the verb specifies in a general way what is taught and may specify the person to be taught.

This is the classical approach to teaching an organised body of knowledge such as 'Geography', 'Literature', or 'Algebra'. Subject teachers, teachers such as university professors concerned with older students and also traditionalists in the teaching profession usually express their objectives in this way. With objectives of this kind you need to do some probing to make them more specific.

First try to get an exact description of the content of what is to be taught. What exactly is meant by 'adjust', by 'map reading', or by 'the importance of group dynamics'? What do these terms include or exclude? Next find out what is expected of the learner. Should he just know about these things, or is he expected to be able to do something?

Experiential objectives

Some teachers view the teaching process as the creation of a stimulating environment which leads to learning. Although the learning experience may be constructed in such a way as to guide the student towards certain objectives, essentially the student is encouraged to explore the learning experience in his own way and to discover his own solutions.

Objectives of this kind may be stated like this:

Provide the student with a map and a situation where, by working out how to use the map, he can discover a 'treasure'.
Organise a situation where people can discover for themselves how to adjust a television receiver.
Give the student experience of different situations in which group dynamics take place so that he can seek the principles involved.

Find out if the *basic* objective is in what the student discovers, or in the experience itself.

For example, the real objective in the first two examples is that the learner will find out how to use a map or adjust a television receiver. The experiences need to be carefully prepared to encourage outcomes. In the third case, however, it could be that the experience is the real objective. The teacher might feel that a variety of interpretations is possible, that it is desirable that different students should gain different things from the experience. Indeed, you might find that the teacher does not want to specify what the outcome of the experience should be.

In this case get a precise description of the experience the teacher wants. Should it be real or artificial? Will the student participate objectively, by watching examples of group dynamics, or subjectively, by being led into a situation which involves group dynamics?

As you define the experience, keep in mind questions which will help you decide whether these experiences are best initiated by television.

Process objectives

Some teachers feel that what is important is to develop a student's ability to think. They feel that the rapid growth in knowledge and the way knowledge changes and is superseded invalidates the content approach. Instead of learning information which may become outdated, they feel students should learn how to handle (process) the different kinds of information they will receive in life. Objectives of this kind describe the mental processes expected of the student. You can recognise them by terms such as 'problem solving', 'analysing', concept forming', or, less precisely, 'understand', 'know', and 'appreciate'.

Examples:

The eighth grade will understand how to read a map.
The rural communities will know how to adjust television receivers.
The trainee teachers will be able to analyse a situation of Group Dynamics.

It is difficult to describe mental processes with accuracy. Words such as 'understand' and 'appreciate' baffle precise definition though they are processes we know well from our own experience.

You need to probe objectives of this kind to try and get an operational definition of the terms used. Remember, though, that this is not always possible.

32

Behavioural objectives

Behavioural objectives describe the behaviour which shows that something has been learned and the context in which the behaviour takes place.

For example:

Given a map and a compass the student will demonstrate map orientation by pointing out five landmarks in alignment with their position on the map.

Given the community television receiver, linked to a power supply and a correctly adjusted aerial, the subject will adjust the receiver to obtain good reception of the rural broadcast.

Given an example of group dynamics the trainee teacher will classify the examples of expected behaviour.

Behavioural objectives ignore the mental processes implied by such terms as 'understand', 'appreciate', etc. Learning is not regarded as having taken place unless there is some evidence to prove it.

Objectives of this kind are clear, specific, and measurable. They are an excellent base for planning. At times, however, the search for precision in the preparation of such objectives results in the exclusion of factors which are imprecise but may have considerable value. For example, should it not be an objective that students *enjoy* map orientation or that trainee teachers are so interested in the basics of group dynamics that they *want to experiment and learn more*?

Make sure that the use of behavioural objectives does not exclude outcomes which involve feelings, emotions, and individuality. These are areas in which television can be effective.

The different kinds of objectives and the different schools of teaching they reflect are not always distinct from each other. Many teachers would say that they applied the principles of more than one school of teaching, and their objectives would reflect this. You can expect to be given any of these types of objectives or a mixture of them.

It is useful to think of any objective as being at some point between the extremes of 'experience' and 'behaviour'. At one extreme the object is to provide an experience. The effect it will have on the audience is not considered. At the other extreme is a behavioural objective which is not related to content. For this, you can use any content you wish in order to achieve the desired behaviour.

Example 1:
A television programme for surgeons shows a new open heart surgery technique. There are no behavioural objectives. The individual surgeon may think what he pleases. One surgeon may decide to adopt the technique; another may decide that it is too dangerous, and that there

33

*are a lot of unanswered questions. Whatever use the individual sur-
geon makes of the experience is his own concern.*

Example 2:
*A television series to teach literacy. The objective is that the audience
will be able to read. What techniques the producer uses, what content
the programme has, do not in themselves matter, as long as the skill
of reading is achieved by the viewers.*

Most objectives fall between these extremes and are a mixture of
the content of the television message and the effect of the message.

Example

Task

as given: "Make a programme for fourteen year olds about the use of forests in this
country"

Next Stage:

Determine Outputs

Entry level:	Can read maps, know layout of country in general terms
Age range:	13.6 to 14.6
Socio economic factors:	Upper working class to middle professional
Educational level:	Primary plus three years secondary
Linguistic factors:	Local accents, but understand language of capital
Motivation:	Required by school syllabus
Reception:	Closed – TV classrooms – broadcast system
Physical context:	TV classroom, 40 odd in room. Untrained monitor present.
Media context:	Have textbook, posters supplied
Programme objective:	After viewing the programme, the student can associate the forest areas of the country with the national economic resources.
Supra-objective:	After viewing the series of programmes, the student can identify the economic resources of the country.

Next Stage:

Make Hierarchy of Objectives

Objectives and short list Components of possible TV strategies
of processes

Given map, identify
forest areas

Motivate	
Explain	Picture: map and areas. Sound: Explain action: add areas
Code	"Northern wood"
Test	Picture: map Sound: Where are forests? Action: none

Given trees, identify
those with useful wood

Explain	Pictures: useful tree, useless tree Sound: Explain:
Code	Code: Thick trunks good wood
Test	Pictures: Various trees Sound: Identify action: none

34

```
Given tree, identify
number of men
          Explain       Picture: Two lumberjacks  Sound: Talk of work  Action: none

Given tree and tools
identify tools needed
          Explain       Picture: Tools used Sound:  Noise they make ?  Action: dem.

Given tree, identify
cutting method
          Explain       Picture: Men and tools cutting tree  Action: cutting tree
                        Sound: effects

Associate forest areas
with economics
          Explain       Picture: Trunk taken away, men given money ?
                        Action: as above  Sound: natural
```

Design teaching strategies

You now know *who* ... will learn *what* ... *in what context.*

Now you need to know what you must teach in order that the instructional objectives of the programme may be achieved. The processes involved are fundamental. Although you may rely on educationalists in this part you must understand the processes, as they are basic to the design of the programme.

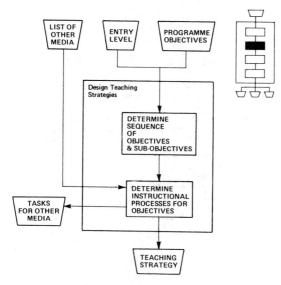

Design teaching strategies.

Determine sequence of objectives

In this process you are working out the stages by which the audience will progress from what they already know to what they need to know, to achieve the objectives of the programme.

Look again at the following task:

A community development project in a rural area is based on new techniques of farming which will be taught by television. The rural community does not yet have television receivers, but sets will be supplied. Produce a programme with the object of teaching the target audience how to adjust their receivers.

Your primary concern, as producer, is with the programme objectives. For each programme objective you should ask, 'What does the audience need to know or be able to do in order to achieve this?'

In the example, in order to adjust a television receiver the audience must be able to:

– *switch on* the receiver
– *select* the correct channel
– *adjust* the brightness, contrast, fine tuning, and volume controls.

These are sub-objectives of the first objective. (They are also called enabling objectives). Each of these new objectives has sub-objectives, and so on. They can be represented on a diagram as a *hierarchy of objectives.*

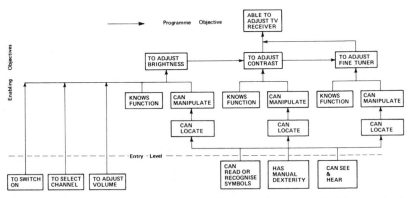

Hierarchy of objectives for programme on 'How to adjust your television receiver'.

The diagram is an attempt to create a hierarchy of objectives for the programme. The diagram could be continued 'downwards' almost indefinitely, but there comes a point where either:

the audience already knows this, or:

the audience must know this in order to use the programme.

36

In each case you have now reached the entry level of the audience. In the second case the use of the programme must be limited to those who have achieved the 'lower' sub-objectives, and these are called 'pre-requisites' for using the programme. A programme on speed-reading would have as pre-requisites that the audience already knows how to read. One on quantum mechanics might have pre-requisites of skills in handling differential equations, knowledge of kinetics, and so on.

In the example, the audience for the programme *How to Adjust your Television Receiver* could already switch on a television receiver, select the correct channel and adjust the volume control. They had learned these from another programme. The objectives of the previous programme thus formed part of the entry level for this programme. The objectives of any programme may thus be sub-objectives (and part of the entry level) for a further programme. The objectives of each programme in a series may be sub-objectives for the objectives of the series. In the example, *why* should the audience learn how to adjust a television receiver? The answer is, firstly, in order that the audience should be able to learn new techniques of farming. This is the desired output of a series of programmes.

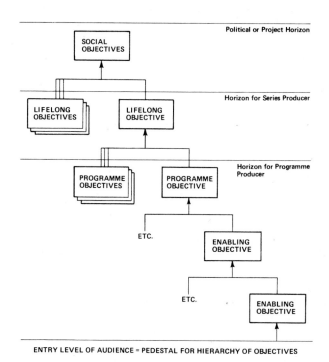

Relationships between objectives.

You may meet what are called *'Life-long objectives'*. These refer to the application of what is learned to real life. In this case the application of the new farming techniques by the individual viewer is a life-long objective. Life-long objectives are achieved by individuals. Social objectives are changes brought about by the contributions of many individuals. The application of the new farming techniques will contribute to a better life for the community – a social objective.

As producer, your primary concern is with the programme objectives. For each objective, ask the question 'what does the viewer need to know in order to learn this?' Repeat the question for each new objective, and write the results out in the form of a hierarchy. Continue the process until you reach the entry level of the audience. The result is a *hierarchy of objectives* for your programme.

Find out why the audience should learn the programme objectives. The answers are the objectives for which you are teaching a sub-objective. They may be lifelong or social objectives, and should be kept in mind while you make your programme.

Next, draw up a draft list of the programme sub-objectives in the order in which they should be achieved. This is a commonsense approach. Do not introduce any objective before any of its sub-objectives. Here is a draft for the television receiver example:

SEQUENCE OF OBJECTIVES FOR THE PROGRAMME
'How to adjust your TV receiver'

In front of each objective read 'Given a television receiver in good condition, linked to a power supply and a correctly adjusted aerial, at a time when a signal is being transmitted, the audience will be able to:

1. Locate the brightness control by touch
2. Rotate the control
3. Explain the function of the brightness control
4. Rotate the control to find the best level of whiteness
5. Locate the contrast control by touch
6. Rotate the control
7. Explain the function of the contrast control
8. Rotate the control to find the best level of contrast
9. Locate the fine tuner
10. Rotate the fine tuner
11. Explain the function of the fine tuner
12. Rotate the fine tuner to obtain the best possible picture
13. Adjust the controls of the TV receiver to obtain the best possible pictures and sound for a given channel

And, for the forestry programme:

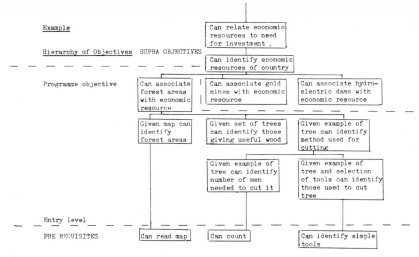

Example

Hierarchy of Objectives   SUPRA OBJECTIVES

	Can relate economic resources to need for investment .
	Can identify economic resources of country

Programme objective

Can associate forest areas with economic resource	Can associate gold mines with economic resource	Can associate hydro-electric dams with economic resource
Given map can identify forest areas	Given set of trees can identify those giving useful wood	Given example of tree can identify method used for cutting
	Given example of tree can identify number of men needed to cut it	Given example of tree and selection of tools can identify those used to cut tree

Entry level

PRE REQUISITES

Can read map	Can count	Can identify simple tools

Student should be able:

1. Given map, to identify forest areas
2. Given set of trees, to identify those giving useful wood
3. Given example of tree, to specify number of men needed to cut it
4. Given example of tree and selection of tools, to identify those suited to cut the tree
5. Given example of tree, to specify method used for cutting
6. To recognise forest areas as economic resource

Now, examine your draft list. In the receiver example, are there any steps which are not really essential, or are so simple that they do not need teaching? Could 'rotate the control' be omitted? Or must this process be taught? For each control?

Is the list very long? Is it reasonable to think of achieving all these objectives in one programme. Your revised sequence of sub-objectives is the output of this process.

If you are given an experiential objective, ask the following:

1. What are the pre-requisites for interpreting the experience?

It is of little value to present an excerpt from a classical drama to an audience that does not understand the language or the allusions it contains. In this case, study the drama and ask, 'Will the audience be able to understand this?' If the answer is 'no', discuss with experts whether to prefix the programme with explanations, whether to attempt to simplify the drama, whether to enact it in a particularly lucid way, or whether to limit the programme to those who will understand (i.e. those having the necessary pre-requisites).

2. What are the elements of the experience?

Some experiences can be very heterogeneous. For example, one

39

producer is given the following experiential objective for an audience of six year olds:

Show what Christmas was like a hundred years ago for a small child living in the English countryside in a poor home.

Think how may elements are involved here:
weather
appearance of the countryside
appearance of the inside of a house
transport
decorations in the house
food
games
Christmas presents
and so on.
Each of these elements has its own sub-elements:
weather
cold
ice
snow
and so on.

You may have to do research into the subject. From the research, the list of what could be included in the programme will grow longer and longer. In the end you will have far too long a list and will have to decide what are the most important elements which can be presented by television.

If the elements of the experience are disjointed or fragmented the experience will be confusing. In determining the sequence of elements in an experience, find a theme, a logic, or a story; something that gives an internal cohesion to the experience.

Determine instructional processes

Now you must find the instructional processes by which each sub-objective is achieved. Go through the list of subobjectives asking, 'How do I teach this?' Do this with the person on your team who is a specialist in teaching methodology. You will probably find that some of the processes of instruction are not suitable for television. Allocate these to more appropriate media if possible. The list of the remaining processes, those assigned to television, in the order in which they should be carried out, is the ouput of this process.

Learning depends on external stimuli and on internal processes in the learner.[1] Teaching or instruction is the process of organising

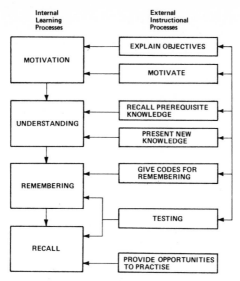

Internal Learning Processes	External Instructional Processes

MOTIVATION
- EXPLAIN OBJECTIVES
- MOTIVATE

UNDERSTANDING
- RECALL PREREQUISITE KNOWLEDGE
- PRESENT NEW KNOWLEDGE

REMEMBERING
- GIVE CODES FOR REMEMBERING
- TESTING

RECALL
- PROVIDE OPPORTUNITIES TO PRACTISE

Determine instructional processes suitable for television and allocate those that are not suitable to other media.

stimuli which will promote learning. The organising of such stimuli is an instructional process. Learning is a complicated and little understood process which appears to have several phases. First, the learner should want to learn. *Motivation* may not be essential but it greatly facilitates learning. Next comes *understanding*. Exactly how this happens is not known. Perception is involved and a process of making sense of what is perceived. Finding a relationship with what is already known is probably an important factor. If what has been understood is to be of long term use it has to be *remembered*, i.e. stored in the brain for future use. What has been understood and remembered is only of real value if it can be *recalled*. The learner needs to be able to take what has been learned out of storage and use it. These phases are necessary to achieve any instructional objective.

Instructional processes for motivation

A learner may already be motivated. Trainee teachers watch a programme on group dynamics because they want to be able to use the techniques. A car owner switches on a programme about car

---

1. See GAGNE, R. M., BRIGGS, L. J., *Principles of Instructional Design*, Holt, Rinehart and Winston, 1974, for a detailed explanation of the relationship between these processes and instructional design.

maintenance because he wishes to be able to service his own car. In such situations confirm that what the programme is going to teach is what the viewer wants to learn. *State the objectives of the programme to the viewer.*

Sometimes, the learners have no initial interest in learning. The audience for the programme on how to adjust a television receiver may be quite satisfied with the low quality images that they are getting. The idea of map reading arouses little enthusiasm in most twelve-year olds.

In this case you need to *motivate your audience.* Arousing enthusiasm, interest, expectancy, a desire to see what follows are things that can be done very well by television.

Instructional processes for understanding

1. *Remind the viewer of the prerequisite knowledge.* You are going to explain or show something which the learner does not as yet understand. Lead him from the known to the unknown. Find what is relevant in his existing knowledge to which he can anchor[2] the new knowledge.

2. *Present the new knowledge clearly.* You are directing attention. Eliminate distraction. Help the learner perceive selectively. Give a variety of examples or repeat in a different way.

Instructional processes for remembering and recall

Give codes to help the learner remember. For example, to help the learner remember the function of the Brightness control you might suggest 'bright gives white'. Some glider pilots are taught the contents of a take-off check by the mnemonic CISTRS (pronounced 'sisters') which helps them remember:

C   Controls - fully free
I   Instruments - gyro caged, altimeter set zero
S   Spoilers – open and in line, closed
T   Trim – set
R   Release - serviceable
S   Straps – secure

This book uses the mnemonic FASTDOTS (see pages 58, 137).

---

2. For the theory behind this concept, see Ausubel, D. P., *Educational Psychology: A Cognitive View*, Holt, Rinehart and Winston, 1968.

If you are teaching something to do with physical phenomena you can:

Show the actual phenomena

Show a diagram which reduces the phenomena to a basic shape

Give a simple symbol or word for remembering the phenomena. [3]

This gives a sequence which takes the learner from understanding to remembering.

Testing shows if understanding has taken place. If it has not, then the instructional processes can be re-cycled. If learning has taken place then testing helps remembering and recall. The satisfaction which comes from responding successfully to a test is thought to have a strong effect on reinforcing what has been learned. If this is true, it makes sense to break down what is to be learned into small units which are easy to learn and test at the end of each unit. A hierarchy of objectives breaks a subject down into small units and permits this approach. Testing techniques work well by television when responses can be formulated quickly. Testing which is related to individualised instruction or testing of a precision performance (e.g. typewriting) or complex skills (e.g. writing an essay) are processes not well suited to television.

It is not always sufficient to learn and remember. Unless what has been learned is used from time to time it is in danger of being forgotten. There must be *opportunities to practise* what has been learned. You can provide these in the programme itself or in later programmes.

Are all these instructional processes necessary? This depends on the learner. An intelligent, self-motivated learner may have developed his own personal techniques for understanding, remembering and recalling. All he needs is the basic experience – the content from which he will learn. Educational programmes for such people have experiential objectives. There is no need to consider instructional processes other than those for understanding. On the other hand, viewers who have not had much schooling, are not accustomed to learning for themselves, and are not very motivated, will need careful attention paid to each of the instructional processes.

Design television strategies

In this process you will look for ways in which the teaching strategy can be implemented by television. It is the crucial stage in which you 'translate' an instructional process into a television process. Your role

3. For the theory behind this theory of understanding, read Bruner, J., Goodnow, J. J., Austin, G. A., *A Study of Thinking*, New York Science Editors, 1967.

TEACHING STRATEGY	
OBJECTIVES ➝	INSTRUCTIONAL PROCESSES
ADJUST T.V. RECEIVER	STATE OBJECT. MOTIVATE RECALL
LOCATE BRIGHTNESS CONTROL	PRESENT CODE TEST
ROTATE	PRESENT
FUNCTION OF BRIGHT. CONTROL	PRESENT CODE
FIND BEST LEVEL OF WHITENESS	PRESENT CODE TEST
LOCATE CONTRAST CONTROL	PRESENT CODE TEST
ROTATE CONTRAST	PRESENT
FUNCTION OF CONTRAST	PRESENT CODE TEST
FIND BEST LEVEL OF BLACK	PRESENT CODE TEST
LOCATE FINE TUNER	PRESENT CODE TEST
ROTATE	PRESENT
FUNCTION OF FINE TUNER	PRESENT CODE TEST
FIND BEST PICTURE	PRESENT CODE TEST
ADJUST T.V. RECEIVER	RECALL PRESENT CODE TEST PRACTISE

A teaching strategy for programme on adjusting the television receiver.

	Objective	*Processes*
1.	Given map, to identify forest areas.	Motivate Explain Code Test
2.	Given a set of trees, to identify those giving useful wood.	Explain Code Test
3.	Given example of tree, to identify number of men needed to cut it.	Explain
4.	Given example of tree and selection of tools to identify those needed to cut tree.	Explain
5.	Given example of tree, to identify method used for cutting.	Explain
6.	Associate forest areas with economic resources.	Explain

44

as a television producer now becomes central, but you should work as a team with your educationalists.

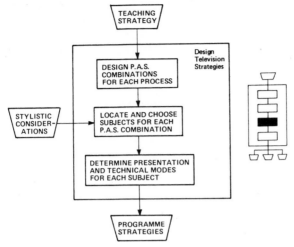

Design television strategies.

For an instructional process to take place, something must *happen* to affect the learner. A teacher may say something; somebody may write something on a blackboard; a reader may look at something on a printed page. What is presented to the learner, or what happens to the learner is the *stimulus* for learning, and may take many forms. If *television* is to be used for teaching it can provide one or more of the following stimuli:

A moving picture
A still picture
A sound.

Design PAS combinations for each process

'P.A.S.' sounds for picture, action, sound. Take each instructional process in your teaching strategy and ask:

What is the key picture for this process?
What is the key action for this process?
What is the key sound for this process?

The combination of picture, action, and sound forms a *stimulus* for the viewer, and you must construct these stimuli so that the objectives of the programme are met.

You will find that there is a tendency to think of these stimuli in terms of *words*, that is, as things to be written and said. However, if what is needed for the instructional process can be expressed entirely

TEACHING STRATEGY →		TELEVISION		
OBJECTIVES →	INSTRUCTIONAL PROCESSES →	T.V. STIMULI		
		KEY PICTURE	KEY SOUND	KEY ACTION
ADJUST T.V. RECEIVER	STATE OBJECT. MOTIVATE RECALL	GOOD T.V. PICTURE " " " CONTROLS THEY KNOW	STATE OBJECTIVE EXPLAIN IT'S POSSIBLE STATE WHAT THEY KNOW	GETTING A GOOD PICTURE SWITCHING ON, CHANNEL & VOL.
LOCATE BRIGHTNESS CONTROL	PRESENT CODE TEST	BRIGHT C ON RECEIVER SYMBOL ON CONTROL A T.V. RECEIVER	QUESTION	DRAW ATTENTION SHOW ANSWER
ROTATE	PRESENT	BRIGHTNESS CONTROL		ROTATE
FUNCTION OF BRIGHTNESS	PRESENT CODE	T.V. PICTURE WORDS	EXPLAIN	SHOW EFFECTS OF BRIGHTNESS
FIND BEST LEVEL OF WHITENESS	PRESENT CODE TEST	T.V. PICTURE & CONTROL TEST CARD " "	EXPLAIN EXPLAIN ASK ONE OF VIEWERS TO TRY—CUE	GETTING BEST WHITE
LOCATE CONTRAST CONTROL	PRESENT CODE TEST	CONTRAST C ON RECEIVER SYMBOL ON CONTROL A T.V. RECEIVER	QUESTION	DRAW ATTENTION SHOW ANSWER
ROTATE	PRESENT	CONTRAST CONTROL		ROTATE
FUNCTION OF CONTRAST	PRESENT CODE	T.V. PICTURE WORDS	EXPLAIN	SHOW EFFECT OF CONTRAST
FIND BEST LEVEL OF BLACK	PRESENT CODE TEST	T.V. PICTURE & CONTROL TEST CARD TEST CARD	EXPLAIN EXPLAIN ASK A VIEWER TO TRY GIVE CUES	GETTING BEST BLACK
LOCATE FINE TUNER	PRESENT CODE TEST	FINE TUNER ON RECEIVER C.U. CONTROL A T.V. RECEIVER	QUESTION	DRAW ATTENTION SHOW ANSWER
ROTATE	PRESENT	FINE TUNER		ROTATE
FUNCTION OF FINE TUNER	PRESENT CODE	T.V. PICTURE WORDS		SHOW EFFECT OF FINE TUNER
FIND BEST PICTURE	PRESENT CODE TEST	PICTURE & FINE TUNER TEST CARD TEST CARD	EXPLAIN EXPLAIN ASK A VIEWER TO TRY	GETTING BEST PICTURE
ADJUST T.V. RECEIVER	RECALL PRESENT CODE TEST PRACTISE	} T.V. RECEIVER } & CONTROLS STATE SEQUENCE } TEST } CARD	DESCRIBE SEQUENCE OF ACTIVITIES STATE TASK & GIVE CUES. STATE TIME OF REPEAT	SHOW HOW TO ADJUST A RECEIVER AUDIENCE ADJUSTS RECEIVER

P.A.S. combinations for each process, for television programme on adjusting receiver.

in words then television is not really needed. Words can usually be transmitted to the learner in other, more economic ways, such as by radio or the printed word. You will have to discuss this problem with your educationalists, because many curricula have been written in such a way that only verbal information is included. However, educationalists are aware of this problem, as they have observed the danger of students learning 'words' off by heart without understanding the concepts involved. This is one of the reasons why the trend in curricular reform is in the opposite direction, and television can play a great part in bringing important experiences to the viewer, often without the use of words.

The first question is about the 'key picture'. You may not need words. (Think, for example, what can be gained by a viewer watching a sequence of pictures about life in a pond). If you do, then normally they should supplement the picture (Where is the pond? How deep is the water? What time of year is it?)

Unfortunately, much television for education is done the opposite way. A written script is first prepared, containing all the words that will be spoken in the programme, and attempts are made to 'visualise it'. The producer takes the script from an educationalist and thinks up pictures to go with the words – 'some graphics here, some film there, a little dramatic scene to liven this up'. What he is doing is illustrating

46

an instructional process that in fact depends entirely on words, and the pictures are relatively unimportant.

At this stage leave *specific* words out. Simply note the essence of what is said – e.g. 'Explain how it works' 'Describes' etc. Except in the special case where drama is involved, specific words will be included at a later stage when the script is written *after* you have decided on the pictures.

To be able to decide what pictures and sounds are to be used, you need to know something of the characteristics of television picture and sound, so the next section of the book is about these.

4 Characteristics of TV systems

Technical limitations: picture definition

A television picture is a *low definition* system – that is, its ability to show detail is very limited. A factor which causes confusion is that the definition of the picture is different at different stages in the system. A cameraman may see, in his viewfinder, a picture that is of slightly higher definition than the producer sees on his studio monitors. The videotape machines and videocassette machines used in some closed-circuit installations produce a lower definition picture on playback, so the viewer sees a picture that is of lower definition than the picture seen by either the producer or the cameraman. They may both see details in the picture that are lost before they reach the viewer. A broadcast system usually has videotape machines that lose little if any definition, but transmission over great distances results in a loss of definition, and most receivers are incapable of producing a high definition picture. Again, the viewer looks at a picture with lower definition than that seen by the producer and the cameraman. Details that they can see in the picture may not reach the viewer.

It is most important that you have a good idea of the definition that can be obtained in your system. Put a test card in front of a camera, so that the image of the card just fills the screen. Have a studio monitor connected to the output of the camera, and look carefully at the result. Identify the finest lines that can be distinguished. Now go back to the card itself, and look directly at the lines you have identified. Was much detail lost in the system? Look at the monitors in the control room, and at the camera viewfinder. Which give the best definition? Which the lowest?

You have been looking at the best possible definition of your system. Your audience will view a lower quality picture, and you need an idea of how good *their* picture is.

Arrange to have the same test card transmitted to the viewing areas in your system, and observe the result on a typical receiver in typical viewing conditions. Can the same amount of detail be seen as before? How much is lost?

Look carefully at any writing that appears on the screen during a programme. Can it be easily read? If you are transmitting for schools, watch the programme in a viewing classroom. What is the smallest letter size that can be used so as to be certain that a pupil at the back of the classroom can read it?

As producer, you must take great care that vital teaching information is not lost on its way to the viewer. Remember that even if you can see detail clearly on the equipment in the studio system, this does not necessarily mean that the audience can see it equally clearly. Pay frequent visits to reception areas so that you can bear in mind the standard of reception when making your programmes. Try to get a sense of how much detail can be shown successfully. Whenever you

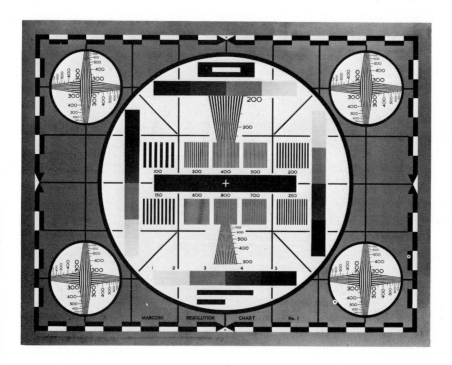

The definition that can be obtained in your system can be assessed by putting a test card in front of a camera and checking the line resolution.

have to show something that contains fine detail, remember that if you try to show all the detail at once, it will be lost on the screen. You usually need show only a few details at a time and should use as much of the screen area as possible to show these details.

Safe area

Most studio monitors and camera viewfinders are adjusted so that the picture does not fill the screen. Normally, however, a viewer's receiver is adjusted so that the picture 'overfills' the screen and some of the picture information is then lost.

In the plate on page 49 you can see that, although the cameraman could see all the test card in his viewfinder, a lot of it was lost by the receiver.

If all the receivers in the system are under your control, as in a closed-circuit system or a well-controlled schools' system, you can arrange to eliminate this problem entirely by having all the receivers adjusted to 'underfill' their screens. In a broadcast system you can arrange to transmit a test card each day which clearly indicates the edges of the transmitted picture (say, by a chequerboard pattern) and

To check the quality of the picture actually seen by your audience use the same test card and observe the result in typical viewing conditions.

tell the people who are responsible for the sets that they should be able to see these edges.

However, in most broadcasting conditions the extent to which receivers will be 'overfilling' their screens is difficult to predict and impossible to control. Thus it is not possible to give a completely trustworthy rule as to how much of the television picture can be safely used for vital information without the risk of its being 'cut off' by the receiver. A figure of 80% is commonly quoted for what is called the 'safe area' or 'essential area'. Some stations mark off a 'safe area' on some or all of their monitors, and use this as a continuous guide as to where important information can be placed. You can quickly and safely mark a monitor in this way by using opaque sticky tape.

Do not be misled into thinking that anything outside the safe area will *not* be seen by the viewer. It *may* not, but some of the area outside the safe area will be seen on *some* receivers.

To repeat, check that in each picture, the essential teaching information is inside the 'safe area' – arbitrarily taken as the middle 80% of the total picture area.

Colour and grey scale

Does your system produce colour pictures? Do all the viewers have colour receivers? If the answers to both these questions are yes, it is worth finding out how 'faithful' your system is. First, compare the colour of an object in the studio with its image on a monitor. Compare this with a typical receiver in the usual viewing conditions. Compare the colours on a slide projected on a screen and as shown by the telecine system. In this case the colour has been modified *twice*, and may have become very different from the real colours of the thing you are showing. This problem can lead to misconcepts of colour. Medical schools using colour television have encountered problems when trying to teach recognition of, for example, skin conditions, where colour recognition is critical.

Find out if adjusting the controls of the receivers changes the colours. Are all the receivers in the system correctly adjusted?

If some or all of the receivers give a black and white picture, you will have to use a picture that is in various shades of grey to give information about a *coloured* world.

In chemistry, the difference between red litmus indicator (indicating an acid solution) and blue litmus (indicating an alkali) is very clear to the naked eye. A television system producing a monochrome result translates the red and blue into the same shade of grey, and the information is completely lost. A 'stills' photographer would solve the problem by means of coloured filters on his camera lens, but such filters are not usually found on television cameras. You might use a commentary like 'you can't see this, but it's red' but this is denying the viewer the experience that the television programme was designed to give. A better solution is to modify the experiment – in this case to choose another indicator. The indicator phenolphthalin is less frequently used in the laboratory; it is red in alkali and colourless in acid. This change can be clearly seen on black and white television.

When you are trying to show something by black and white television which depends on distinguishing different shades of grey, remember that a studio monitor distinguishes many more shades of grey than does the receiver.

Use a more 'contrasty' picture than you would if the viewer were watching a studio monitor.

Another difference between the studio monitor and the viewer's receiver that you must bear in mind is their different reaction to 'brightening' or 'darkening' the picture.

When a monitor receives less signal* the total picture darkens. If no extraneous light is falling on the screen reducing the signal to its limit makes the screen go completely black (both producer and engineer commonly call this 'going to black'). On most television *receivers*, however, the effect is different. The change is then not one of brightness but of *contrast*. On the receiver the white parts of the picture become grey, and *so do the black parts*. When the signal has been reduced to its limit, the result is a grey screen, not a black one. When bright white titles are added to a scene, the effect on the receiver is to increase total contrast.

The scene to which the titles were added gets darker on the receiver, but stays the same on the monitor.

Be careful not to suddenly introduce very bright areas into a picture. If a bright reflection is suddenly given off by a piece of jewellery, if a flame is lit, or if a title is superimposed, the rest of the viewer's screen may go darker. Conversely, if you want to give the effect of a dark street, for example, it is no use just reducing the level of illumination – in this case you need some bright spots – lamplight shining through hair, 'moonlight' reflected in a puddle – in order to keep the rest of the screen dark.

Shape distortion

A maladjusted television receiver can distort shapes.

On one occasion, when a television teacher was explaining the con-

*The signal is the electrical voltage that controls the brightness of part of the picture at any moment. For a full description, see Millerson, G. *The Technique of Television Production*, or any textbook for television engineers.

cept of a triangle, because a classroom receiver was badly adjusted, triangles appeared on the screen with curved lines. After the programme, the students reproduced triangles with the same curved lines. When straight lines are not involved, the eye/brain seems able to accept quite a lot of distortion of this kind without difficulty, and the problem only really arises in shapes whose symmetry is important. Transmitted circles, in particular, rarely appear as circles on the screen of the receiver, and noticeable distortion occurs on squares as well.

Sound

The sound that reaches the viewer is usually poor. Technically, the studio system may produce high quality sound, but the small size of the receiver's loudspeaker severely limits the quality, and often the quantity, of the reproduced sound. In addition, no classroom is ever entirely silent.

Avoid severe changes in the intensity of sound being used. Do not convey essential information by low level sound – by whispers in a drama, for example.

Stereo sound is almost unknown in television – though many videotape machines and videocassette units have two audio channels – all the sound comes to the viewer from a single sound source, the loudspeaker. The sound may well *appear* to come from the position of the speaker on the screen, but this is the same illusion as tht used by a ventriloquist. It means, incidentally, that anybody can be a ventriloquist – if the speaker does not appear on the screen. If the puppet on the screen is moving its mouth realistically, the illusion is immediate!

Lack of size information

There is a story of a television station that made a determined attack on the problem of malaria eradication. A well budgeted programme for rural, humid areas showed in great detail the action of the anopheles mosquito. Viewers were shown the mosquito alighting on human skin, drawing out blood, and injecting the malarial parasite. Further sequences showed the precautions that should be taken, such as protecting water supplies and spraying. The whole programme was carefully and expensively made, and great results were expected. However, evaluation teams found that, even after watching the programme, viewers were making no attempt to put its recommendations into practice.

Oh, yes, they had enjoyed the programme, but, you see, *their* mosquitoes were small ones, not at all like the enormous ones they saw in the programme!

If an object is shown by itself on the television screen, there is no information as to how large it is. Occasionally, as in puppetry or model work, where an illusion is being sought, this is an advantage, but generally it is important that the viewer knows the size of the thing being shown.

To give this information, compare the object with something whose size is well known – a large rocket may be compared with a local building, a micro-organism with the head of a pin, and so on.

Lack of third dimension

Look at the object shown below.

Solids as two dimensions: the true form is not evident from this picture.

Is this object thin and flat, cylindrical, spherical? This gives no information that enables you to answer. Compare with that below, which gives a better impression of the three-dimensional shape of the object.

It is often necessary to show an object from more than one angle to show its shape clearly.

54

This shows its shape much more obviously.

Contradiction or distraction

A picture should *complement* rather than *contradict* the sound message. Here is an example of a contradiction between image and sound that would puzzle many students.

Contradiction or distraction: contradictions of image and sound can mislead the viewer.

The framing of a picture should not be such that the viewer's eye is drawn away from the object to which the sound track is referring. This plate shows a good example of the effect of distraction.

"This tanker holds several thousand gallons of high crude fuel". Distracting image: the framing of a picture should not be such that the viewer's eye is drawn away from the object to which the sound track is referring.

Duplication

Picture	Sound	
	Presenter (off):	Today we are going to look at a tropical island
artwork	Music (under):	*Island in the Sun*
TITLE: Tropical Island		

What is essentially the same message is given in four different ways: *spoken* word (presenter), *written* word (title), *picture* and *music*. There is no evidence that literate adults learn better from a duplicated message like this, but children and illiterate adults can be confused.

Many words shown on television duplicate. The presenter says the word at the same time as it is shown. This can be quite irritating for

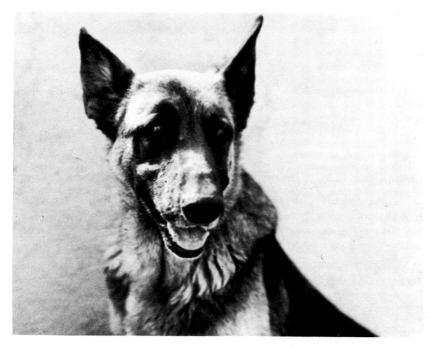

"Do you like dogs?"
One word may be worth a thousand pictures. If the sound carries a *general* concept (e.g. 'dogs'), while the picture shows a *particular* example (e.g. of one dog, perhaps an alarming one), there may be an unintended reaction.

literate adults, particularly when a long sentence is shown. Many people can read faster than a sentence can be read out loud but find that they cannot read ahead of the voice in the programme because they become confused. They are held to the slow pace of the voice which permits them to read the sentence only once.

However, if the audience is not fully literate and would have difficulty in reading or pronouncing the written words, then by saying the words the presenter is *complementing* the picture.

Cueing

Most people are not accustomed to 'reading' a picture with care. In the next example, the spoken word and picture complement each other so that the attention of the student is 'cued' to the elements of the picture which he needs to be able to recognise:

Picture	Sound
Picture of volcano	What kind of mountain is this?
	(5 second pause)
Word "volcano" appears over picture	(2 second pause)
Word disappears	How can you tell it is a volcano? Look at the summit
Zoom in to summit	It appears truncated

Setting

If you are showing the details of something to the viewer – and television is good at this – is it quite clear to him how the detail relates to the whole? It is easy to be so intent on showing the details of the pistons of a locomotive that you never show the complete locomotive, to show details of a pond without ever showing the whole pond, or to confuse the viewer as to where a complete sequence is taking place.

A shot that shows the *visual context* of a sequence is called an establishing shot, and should not be forgotten in your planning.

The limitations – a mnemonic

This book uses a mnemonic – fastdots – when it is necessary to remember the most important of these limitations. FASTDOTS stands for:

F   Fine detail
A   Area lost
S   Size information
T   Third dimension
D   Distraction
O   Opposition (i.e. contradiction)
T   Tints (i.e. colour information)
S   Setting

Resource limitations

Make sure you have a good idea of the capabilities of your television installation. If you have a studio, what is its total floor area? Can it all be lit? Can the lighting of different parts be controlled separately? What is the largest size of object that could be brought into the studio (this is usually decided by the size of the studio doors)? Is there any weight limitation on what the studio floor can stand?

Spend a practice session in the studio to find out the *smallest* area that can fill the screen and still be in focus.

With a zoom lens, this is likely to be with the lens zoomed in at minimum focusing distance.

With a turret camera, the widest angle lens gives the smallest area *if* it is physically possible to get the object close enough to the camera and to illuminate it at the same time. A few cameras can be fitted with supplementary close-up lenses (diopter lenses) which allow the camera to focus closer than usual, and range extenders (or tele extenders) which produce narrower lens angles than usual. Find out if these are available and how long they take to fit.

Can they be put into place and taken off again during the programme, or once fitted will they have to stay in place for the whole programme?

The above exercise is also worth trying with whatever film and still camera you have available.

Find out from your engineers what is the *longest cable* that can be fitted to the television cameras in your studio(s). This may be longer than you expect – a hundred metres (yards) is quite common, and up to five times this is usually possible. Studio microphones, too, can be fitted with long cables, as they are of the 'low impedance' type which permits this.

With long cables fitted to your cameras and microphones, the operation can move out of the studio, while still using the studio control room.

Have a look *around* the area of your studios. Would it be useful to have the cameras in the corridor outside the studio? Can you get them out of doors altogether? Investigate this carefully – you may find some area that will be excellent for some programmes. One television station has an ornamental indoor garden a few hundred feet from one of its studios and has made 'jungle' programmes in it. Another has taken the cameras into the yard outside to show how to change the wheel of a lorry. Another regularly scheduled open air programmes, after the studio lighting grid was accidentally put out of action.

What *mobile* television units are available? How many cameras are available with each unit? what lenses are fitted? Does the unit need an external power supply? These are the factors that determine its production capabilities.

59

Can you make *film*? With or without sound? Can such facilities be hired if necessary?

What sources of ready made material are available? Are there libraries of film, videotape, discs, audiotape, slides, photographs?

5 The planning system – II

Location and choice of subjects

This requires a transition from the general to the particular. If you have decided to use a woodcutter in the programme you now need to think about how to get a particular woodcutter for the purpose. Or, you have decided to show a television receiver – now you start planning how to get a particular receiver. You want the word 'chimborazi' to appear on the screen, you start to plan how to obtain that word for the screen.

This book uses the following classifications for the *subjects* of the P.A.S. combination. Any particular combination will use one or more of these.

1. *People.*
2. *Things.* Animate or inanimate, mobile or fixed, animal, vegetable, or mineral.
3. *Places.* These are often of secondary importance as subject matter – the surroundings or setting for people and things. Places can, however, be the principal subject for pictures, as in a programme on mountains.
4. *Abstractions.* This is information that has to be simplified or symbolised. Drawings of abstract things, written words, numbers maps, diagrams.
5. *Sound.* People, things, and places have their own integral sound. Sound may also be subject matter in its own right: a piece of music, a famous speech, a poem.
6. *Library material.* These are picture, action, sound combinations that already exist – a videotape of part of another programme, a film of an historical event.

7. *Synthetics.* These are pictures or sounds that are generated electronically without the need for external 'subject matter'. Examples are:

Words produced by a character generator.
Patterns produced by pattern generators in a vision mixing desk.
Multiburst.
1khz tone produced by an audio oscillator.

People

You may need people in the programme for one or more of the following purposes:

a. The viewer needs the experience of seeing and/or hearing this particular person. For example, a local celebrity or a visiting professor talks about what he has done, and what his future plans are. An interview with a local policeman may be needed for a social science programme, one with a farmer in a programme on weather, and so on.
Such people, who are selected for a particular instructional process, we shall call 'guests'.
b. How do you show someone who is not available? How do you show Abraham Lincoln, Socrates? One possibility is to use actors. Drama can be a powerful tool for teaching, and can also be used when you need to show a 'situation'. This may be a historical situation 'How did such-and-such happen?' for a history programme, a 'typical' situation – somebody buying something in a shop – for a mathematics or a language programme, or a drama that the viewer needs to know, for a literature programme.
c. The choice of 'things' to be shown in the programme may influence the choice of people to be shown. Is the object to be shown associated with a person? Examples are a fire extinguisher used by a fireman, the tools used by a woodcutter, the hypodermic used by a nurse. Some demonstrations require constant supervision before and after they are shown to the viewer, and require a specialist *demonstrator.*
d. How do you link parts of the programme together? How do you present verbal information? One solution is to have a 'presenter'. A presenter is someone who appears on the television screen and speaks directly to the viewer. He explains what is happening and introduces what is to be seen. Usually he maintains the continuity of the programme. By looking directly at the camera lens, he gives the illusion that he is actually making contact with the viewer, who may greet him as a friend when he appears.

62

The 'television teacher' is a special case of the presenter. Traditionally, the television teacher takes responsibility for the academic content of what is being shown, and is often the one who 'writes' the programme. The danger here is that all concerned in the production think in terms of a 'lesson' that already exists, and assume that all that is necessary is to 'televise' the lesson. This can lead to a sterile form of instructional television, which has the limitations of the classroom lesson and those of television, and the advantages of neither. However, a 'television teacher' who takes part in the planning process as a member of the production team can be most valuable.

e. How do you show a guest? Some guests can effectively address the camera directly, and thus become the 'presenter' for that part of the programme. Usually, however, it is easier if the session is carried out on a question-and-answer basis. Most presenters prefer to do their own interviewing, but it may at times be more convenient to use a separate *interviewer*.

Another example of interaction between people during a programme would be a 'confrontation' between a *studio audience* of farmers and a team of agricultural experts.

Another technique is to have pupils in the studio who are learning at the same time as the viewers. It is claimed that the pace and content of the teaching in the programme can be modified by the presenter 'as he goes along' by reference to the studio pupils. One difficulty with this idea is that the studio pupil is not receiving the same stimulus as the viewer, so his reactions may differ from the viewers'. If the presenter speaks at all to the studio pupils his 'contact' with the viewers is at that moment broken, and the viewer becomes a mere eavesdropper to teaching given to someone else. Attempts to meet these objections have led to programmes in which a sample audience watches and listens to the programme at a place not in the studio, but has microphone and loudspeaker contact with the presenter.

If you need a presenter, a decision that you need to make immediately is whether to use a professional actor or a teacher. The argument as to which to use, has been going on as long as educational television has existed. There are really no rules; much depends on the particular case. In general, you can expect that the professional actor will be able to learn and repeat accurately a written script as word-perfect as is necessary for a complicated production. His delivery will always be clear, and his studio discipline (his ability to stop and start and accept modifications) of a high standard. He will be able to take on such duties as reading the commentary to a film sequence and interviewing without difficulty. However, he is unlikely to be competent in demonstrating complicated pieces of equipment, as would be necessary, for example, in a science programme.

The teacher will not be as word perfect as the actor and he may need training in voice production for television. However, even though he may depart from the written script, he is less likely to make errors of fact in what he says than the actor who knows nothing of the subject. He should be quite at home with demonstrations, and can usually show good technique in this, though he must be taught the changes needed for television. He will be able to participate in the development of the programme, and may well contribute useful ideas of his own.

Your choice should also be influenced by the nature of the target audience. A serious adult audience would be impressed by the fact that Professor X himself is speaking to them and will forgive him his nervous mannerisms. A young audience, on the other hand, is unforgiving of any apparent nervousness and unimpressed by the qualifications of the speaker, but responds quickly to a confident friendly presentation. (This is an example of the stylistic considerations that were an output of the 'determine the outputs' stage. The other considerations, in particular language or dialect, must be borne in mind at this stage.)

If you do intend to use a teacher as a presenter it may be worth making sure that he has professional recognition. Teaching associations are good sources of teachers to be presenters.

For professional actors you should approach an agency. If your resources are limited, drama schools are a possible, but unpredictable, source of talent.

If you use children, you will probably find that unless they are professional child actors they are very unpredictable. The most charming and lively of youngsters will go wooden with rehearsals and few can stand more than 30 minutes of studio lights at a time. If you need a precise performance following a script, then you need a child actor. An intelligent, extrovert child *can* give a good performance if you let him use his own words, give him the idea of what you want and are prepared to accept a free interpretation of what you want. Avoid rehearsals in the studio. The child's *first* performance will be the best one and will steadily deteriorate.

For specific people or specialists your search may take you far afield and may take a long time.

You may be able to select your participants immediately. If you are at all uncertain, set up the studio for a typical programme and try to record a part of the programme using each possible person in turn. You will get a better idea of the effect of each person on the screen if you can arrange for someone else to direct the recordings and you to judge by watching the playback. If you have the time and the resources, play back the recordings to typical audiences to see the effect on them.

If your subject has various roles in the programme – interviewing, commentating, demonstrating – you should include these in the audition. You may find that one candidate can fulfil all roles adequately, or it may be advisable to divide the tasks between different people.

The output of this stage is a list of participants.

How much do you intend to pay the participants? Will this be a once and for all payment, or will further payments become due if the programme is repeated? Will the participant(s) have any expenses? Who will pay these? When are the participants available?

Other information is needed for other departments connected with the programme. Will the participant provide his own wardrobe? Does he give any particular problems to make-up? Do you want his name printed on any of the graphics – if so, what should the precise spelling and wording be? Is any special equipment needed for him to demonstrate? Will he supply this? Will he supply consumables? Will he use other equipment, such as prompting devices?

To determine presentation mode and technical mode for the people you have selected, you must make a series of decisions that are closely interlinked. The flowchart below makes this clear.

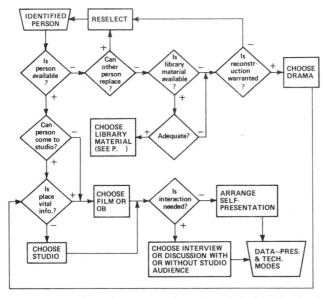

Decision sequence to determine presentation and technical modes for 'People'.

Things

A few kinds of programme – a monologue or a dialogue showing only the participants' faces, a programme on local dances, a current affairs programme – may not need 'things' at all. However, the ability of television to show things is one of its great opportunities for television.

The important archaeological find that is in the national museum can be shown simultaneously to thousands of children who would not normally be able to go to the museum. The latest piece of medical equipment can be shown to all the people who would be interested. An important piece of scientific equipment used in a little-known department of a university can be shown to all who are studying science. There are schools in areas in which local transport is difficult – in these you may well find children who have never seen a ship, and this, too, can be remedied by television.

When you are selecting things, keep in mind the limitations of television – refer to 'FASTDOTS' on page 137.

Do you need to show fine detail? The choice between objects could depend on the ease with which this can be done. The fine graduations on a mercury thermometer are difficult to see, but the bold information on a dial thermometer is much easier.

Choose colours that will easily be distinguished on the screen. If you are in any doubt, take the object you are considering along to the studio and do a test. Often the problems of obtaining sufficient contrast are obvious with a little thought. For example, if you are going to show how to lace an audio tape into a recorder, a brown tape in a brown machine is obviously going to cause difficulties – choose a white tape.

When you are choosing demonstrations for subjects on a school curriculum, bear in mind that the 'usual' demonstrations were originally chosen to be relatively inexpensive, easy to organise and to store, and of a size that fits easily into a classroom or a school laboratory. These constraints do not necessarily apply to you, and you may be able to organise a far more effective demonstration with the resources of television.

Most schools limit the demonstration of a simple barometer to one with 30 inches of mercury. With 30 feet of polythene tubing and a reasonably tall support – perhaps a transmitter tower – you can construct an impressive *water* barometer.

The standard demonstration of the suffocating effect of carbon dioxide is done with a gas jar and some matches. You might persuade the local fire brigade to set light to a pool of inflammable liquid and attack the fire with CO^2 extinguishers.

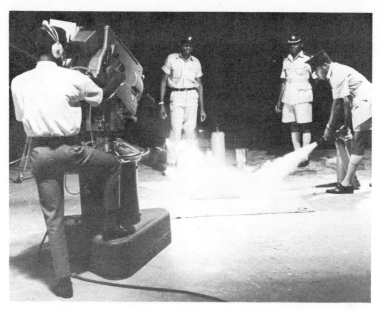

The standard demonstration of the suffocating effect of carbon dioxide is done with a gas jar and some matches. You might persuade the local fire brigade to set light to a pool of inflammable liquid and attack the fire with CO_2 extinguishers.

Most television systems are not as well adapted to showing 'things' as they are to showing people. The primary consideration is thus often the technical mode. You will have to determine the technical mode according to:

1. *The size and accessibility of the 'thing'.*

Is it very large? A ship or a building? A film camera enables you to fly over it, drive around it, or go inside it. A mobile television unit also has possibilities.

Can you get it to the studio but not inside? With long cables you can take cameras and microphones outside the studio. Is it too small for the standard lenses of the cameras? Television and film cameras can look at or through microscopes, particularly those of the projection type. If there is no movement – a petal, a diffraction grating – a photograph may do as well. If there is movement – bacteria for example – film or videotape and select the part you want.

2. *The speed of any movement or change which has to be shown.*

Do you need to distort time? This can be done in five ways:

a. Slowing down the action
b. Speeding up the action
c. Trigger techniques
d. Time distortion by editing
e. Time distortion by photography

a. Use 'slowing down' techniques when the action is too swift to see clearly, such as the technique of a high jump or a discus throw, how a frog's tongue uncoils to catch an insect, or the details of how a drop of water splashes.

Most film cameras can be adjusted to run faster than their normal speed, filming at, say, 64 pictures per second instead of the usual 24. When this is reproduced on a film projector running at standard speed, the effect is to show the motion slowed down, in this case by nearly three times. Special high speed cameras can run at speeds such as 2,000 pictures per second.

Some videotape machines, and a special unit that uses a recording disc, can also give a kind of slow motion effect on playback, though the result usually lacks definition and image quality.

b. If the film camera runs at a slower rate than usual, the result on the screen will be speeded up. Crystal growth, a flower opening, the development and movement of clouds, the construction of a building, can all be shown in this way. Avoid such scenes using human beings – the effect is comical.

c. Wild life films often require days or even weeks of waiting for a particular flurry of action. Either the cameraman must wait patiently for the right moment, or the camera must be operated by a trigger mechanism such as a trip wire.

d. If a process takes too long to be shown conveniently in its entirety, editing techniques offer the possibility of reducing the screen time without speeding up the action that is seen. You can make a sequence showing the beginning of the process, then something connected with, but not part of, the process – say, the operator's face – and then the last part of the process. This technique is much used in film work, and is also possible with some kinds of videotape equipment.

You can leave a television camera with a videotape recorder running for a long period (limited by the duration of the tape) to cover an expected action. Examine the recorded tape at intervals, rewind and start the recorder again until you get the action you want.

e. A 'still' camera chooses and records a particular moment of time. This is then displayed for as long as required. This conversion of a moment into an appreciable period of time is time distortion. For things that remain constant for long periods of time, the distortion may be unnoticeable. A photograph of a pyramid may be indistinguishable from a film or a videotape made at the same place. However, if the view includes a camel walking in front of the pyramid, the difference is obvious.

You can use a 'still' camera to show changes. A series of photographs, one taken each day, of a flower will show its growth, but will not give the effect of continuous smooth movement that can be obtained with a film camera.

If you leave the shutter of a still camera open while the subject it is looking at changes, the camera produces a synthesis of the complete time for which the shutter is left open. Thus all the lightning flashes of a storm can be included in one photograph, the trails of 'moving' stars can be recorded, and so on.

The problems of showing particular objects may lead to the need for using several modes. For example, how would you show the working of the escapement in a watch? To establish where the mechanism was, and its size, you could show the presenter taking off his watch, and perhaps opening it. The interior of the watch is probably too small for the television cameras to show adequately without special techniques, so you next show a film of the interior of the watch, shot with a special close-focusing lens. The working of the escapement still cannot be seen clearly in situ, so next you use a specially made model of the escapement which the presenter can take to pieces and reassemble in the studio .

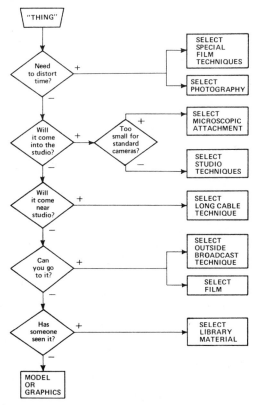

Decisions sequence to determine technical mode for 'Things'.

You may also need to estimate the time and cost aspects etc. in advance: If the thing is to be made, how much time is needed? How many people and what expenditure are involved?

If it is to be bought, what will it cost?

If it is to be borrowed, will there be a fee for this? What transport arrangements are needed? Who is to look after it while it is borrowed? Is insurance necessary? If so, what does it cost?

If it is a demonstration, will it need electricity, gas, or fire precautions?

Places

Your selection of a place as a subject for a scene will be interlinked with technical considerations. The flow chart below shows the process to be followed.

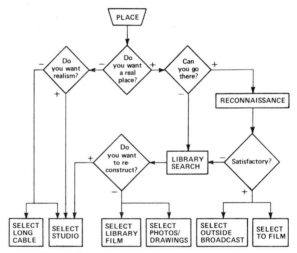

Flow chart for selection of place for a scene.

Never assume, however well you know a place, that you can simply arrive some time with cameras and crew. You must do a *reconnaissance* (recce) beforehand to find out if it is possible to make the sequence there and what you will need in order to do so.

When you do a reconnaissance, take with you:

1. Members of your team – particularly the content specialist.
2. A camera – get a photograph of every scene that you are likely to use. These will help you to plan and explain the place to members of the team who could not come with you. The pictures may even become programme material as credits or for rear projection.
3. A check list.

Is the location suitable? ....
If not, what might make it suitable? ....
Can you get permission to use the location? ....
      From whom? ....
      When? ....
      For how much? ....
What restrictions are involved in using the location? ....
Will you use natural light? ....
If so, at what times will the sun be in suitable position? ....
Will shadows need filling by reflectors or by artificial light? ......
Will camera(s) be able to shoot from suitable positions
without shooting towards sun? ....
If you are to use artificial light, is there sufficient
already installed? ....
Who can switch it on? ....
Will you have to supply artificial light? ....
At what points will you place camera(s)? ....
What camera mounts will you use? ....
What lenses are needed? ....
What microphones are needed? ....
Where will you put the control unit/vehicle? ....
Is there sufficient power for this, and for the lamps, if any? .....
From where can the power be supplied? ....
Who can switch it on? ....
What kinds of sockets are used? ....
What voltages and frequencies are avilable? ....
How much cable must you bring? of what types? ....
Where will you run power cables, microphone cables? ....
Do you need to rope off spectators? ....
If so, who can do this? ....
Can the team be fed on site? How? When? ....

As you decide whether or not to use a location, consider:
Are there other sites which might be better?
How important is an historical site which you need to show 'in its
own time'? Look for recent additions – anomalies – and see if they
can be covered, or if you can arrange your shots to eliminate them.

If you are not satisfied with the results of the reconnaissance, or if
you need to see what the place *used* to look like, search libraries for
old photographs and drawings. This also applies if you could not go
to the place because it was inaccessible or no longer existed.

71

As a result of this search you may decide to use film, photographs, or drawings which you found, or use these pictures as a guide to 'reconstruct' the place. You can make a studio set or a model.

Combinations of people, things and places

The previous sections have dealt with the separate techniques for selecting and planning people, things, and places. Usually you need to find a combination of these, and you have to choose a method that meets the reqirements of all three.

If you need to show a person adjusting a television receiver, perhaps the setting is unimportant and some neutral background will suffice. Alternatively, perhaps a particular audience will identify more with the objectives of the programme if there is a setting similar to that in which they are viewing.

To show how to orientate a map you would need a map and a compass, a person to demonstrate, and a place where you can get good views of the area covered by the map.

If you are not concerned with a *particular* place, do you need a setting that is realistic or one that is abstract or unrealistic?

For the abstract or unrealistic, the studio is probably the best place. However, if you need a realistic background, consider the possibilities of 'long cable' techniques. What sort of setting lies outside your studio(s)?

One problem with going outside the studio, whether by using long cables, a television mobile unit, or a film camera, is that the environment is often unpredictable. Curious bystanders have to be roped off, clouds creep up or the sun comes out just as you start shooting, or an aeroplane passes overhead as you open the microphones.

Studios, on the other hand, offer the advantages of a fully controlled environment. The intensity, direction, and quality of light can be controlled easily. The studio is usually completely isolated from outside noise, and thus the sound produced for the microphones can be completely controlled. Irrelevant details can be eliminated, and a clear background, without distractions, can be provided for each shot. Each part of the programme can be carefully rehearsed and repeated as many times as necessary.

Find out what facilities for sets are available at your station.* Can sets be made to order? Is there a scene dock of scenery items that can be selected and used? Some stations keep a 'standard' set installed in the main studio, and this is seen with monotonous regularity in

*See, eg., Millerson *Technique of Television Production* pp. 134-167, on scenery for television studios.

programme after programme. Even a standard set, though, can be modified. If the station has a scenic designer, discuss your programme requirements with him, and spend some time in the studio with him so that you get a good idea of what needs to be installed, and where.

You will need to *estimate*:
How much money is needed for mobile or film units.
How much the sets will cost to make or to rent.
When could these be ready/available.
Who needs to be paid, and how much.
A demonstration, is a combination of people, things, and place.
The check list for the demonstration is:
What will be demonstrated?
How long does the operation take?
What consumables does it need?
Are there restrictions as to when it can take place?
Who will do it?
When will he/she/they be available?
Will anyone need to be paid? How much?
For *filming* a demonstration:
Can the demonstration be broken down into repeatable sections?
Can the operation be repeated to order?
What cutaways are possible?
For all filming:
What camera with what motor will you use? (The longest necessary duration of shot is what you need to know to decide this.)
How much film will be needed?
Of what type?
Do you need to record sound?
Sync. or wild?
What recorder will you take, if any?
How much audio tape will be needed, if any?

Abstractions

If you are trying to show words, numbers, diagrams, maps, or pictures that have no movement, then you should question whether they belong in your programme. Much instructional television is part of a media combination (page 29) that includes print. Printed graphic material is usually much clearer than a television image. It also has the advantage that it can be looked at over and over again and studied at the speed of the individual. For a series of programmes about a particular country, a poster could be provided with a detailed map of the country for reference. If teacher's notes are provided for a programme which contains words that will be new to the viewers, the notes can suggest that the teacher write the words on a blackboard before the programme starts. Many systems have the habit of using a superimposition each time a new word is used. This can disrupt a classroom, as pupils attempt to write the new word down.

Still pictures may be useful in television production –

1. When it is necessary to remove motion from a picture – a golfer's swing stopped at one point to show the positions of hands and arm – to show the shape of a lightning flash – to show a building in a busy street without the distraction of traffic moving in front of it.
2. When it is necessary to combine two images and motion is not important – to show the position of the skeleton inside a sperm whale – to show the possible moves or radii of action of players in a ball game – to delineate particular areas in an aerial photograph.
3. When the original material is a still picture – a photograph of a planet – a map – a historical photograph or drawing.
4. To show symbols and diagrams – a mathematical formula, a histogram of economic trends.
5. To show words.

Animated captions may be used:

1. To show a flow or movement
2. To show direction
3. To show progressive development. Many diagrams or pictures are difficult to grasp at first glance, but if they are shown in stages of growing complexity they can become comprehensible.
4. To show the development of mathematical problems or word or sentence structure.

Animated graphic to show 'flow'.

Through cut-outs of rain and evaporation alternate black and white gives effect of movement in correct direction. 'Black crushing' – a camera level adjustment that destroys all details in the 'blacks' – can conceal the mechanism from the viewer. Alternatively, you can use a picture of the animation as the 'Key' in a vision mixing desk which has this facility, and make the colours of the result anything you like. This, too, removes the information about the mechanism from the picture.

The number of *words* that can be put on to a television screen at one time so that your viewers can read them depends on the definition of the complete system, and this is something that you will have to find out. There are a number of 'rules' such as, not to have more than 7 lines, and have each line with no more than 20 letter units (the space between words equals one unit), but your system may be incapable of meeting this requirement, or may be able to do better. Do a series of tests in the worst viewing conditions in your system to find out just how many words can be made legible at once – then write your own 'rule'.

If you need to show more words or numbers than your 'rule' allows, then you should either split them into several captions or use a drum or roller caption, or a graphic pan or tilt.

Does your system have an electronic character generator? Many television stations have one or more of these units so that they can put words on the screen at short notice. If you have one available, find out if the letters it produces are large enough to be read in the worst viewing conditions in your system. Does the unit have a 'memory'? If not, you will need an operator to 'type out' the words during the programme. How long does it take him to replace one 'message' by another?

Does your system have a *'standard size'* for its graphics? When captions are made to a standard size, they can be stacked on stands in the studio and changed quickly by the floor manager or an assistant.

Does your system have 'caption scanners'? These are units with a fixed camera and a support for captions. Some have a zoom lens or a movable camera, and this permits a great variety of material to be used, but then you must assign an operator to the unit for the programme.

If you intend to have parts of the graphic fill the screen – if you are going to pan, tilt, or zoom – each *part* that you intend to show must be of an adequate size.

Very large graphics can be shown on the screen together with the presenter, by making them part of the set. The picture can then be seen as a whole or in parts, and serves as a continuous reminder of a subject. For example, a programme about a city can have a giant map behind the presenter reminding the viewer of the city's size and general shape. The presenter can talk about 'the area west of the river', and stand beside this part of the map, broadly indicating what he means. He can talk about a particular place, followed by a close-up of that part of the map to introduce film of that area. In colour studios 'chroma key' can give a similar effect, using a slide on telecine for the background.

Provided camera movement or animation is not wanted, anything that can be shown on a standard caption can be photographed and made into a *slide* to show on telecine. This releases studio cameras for other shots and eliminates problems of 'lining up' captions.

If your telecine changes smoothly between captions, a simple form of animation is possible.

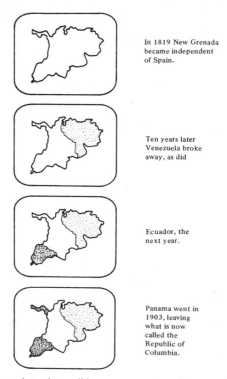

In 1819 New Grenada became independent of Spain.

Ten years later Venezuela broke away, as did

Ecuador, the next year.

Panama went in 1903, leaving what is now called the Republic of Columbia.

Storyboard to show slide sequence appearing as animation.

To make a *filmed graphic sequence* is an expensive process, but may be less costly than taking up valuable studio time. One problem you may face in using such a technique is that the presenter may find it difficult to synchronise his commentary exactly with the changes in caption that occur in the film. To solve this problem, you may decide to edit a separately recorded sound track to match the film sequence.

To create an *animated film* sequence several pictures can be drawn on separate sheets of plastic ('cells') and placed in turn on a master background. Provided the film camera is stopped while each change is made, the viewer will see these changes occur instantaneously in the finished sequence.

To *estimate* all your *graphics requirements* it may be useful to make a chart to list the work for each of several departments that may be involved (e.g. design, photography, film production, studio sets, etc.). See graphics request form page 100.

Sound

For much instructional television, the process of obtaining the sound is intimately bound up with the process for obtaining the picture, and need not be considered separately. Most sound that is obtained separately is re-recorded 'library' material, and there is a section below on this.

It is sometimes convenient to make separate arrangements for recording some of the sound needed for a programme. The following are some examples:

1. *Sound effects*. You may have film of a scene but no appropriate sound. Sound effects records can be helpful here, but it may be more efficient, and probably more appropriate, to record the sound of a similar scene. This can be done using a portable tape recorder. Similarly, when you are filming, it may be useful to record an 'atmosphere' tape.

2. *Pre-recorded soundtrack*. You might include a spoken poem, with illustrations on captions, in your programme, recording the poem beforehand, perhaps in a radio studio and using the tape for the programme, synchronising the caption changes to it. Dialogue, or more complicated sound, can be recorded in the same way. Captions, or even a puppet sequence, can be synchronised to the result.

3. *Music*. If you need music for a programme or a series, you may be able to get exactly what you need, and avoid copyright problems, by arranging to have a group write and perform the music for you. Make sure that they sign a written agreement that your payment to them includes all further use of the recording by you. Make sure, too, if they did not write the music themselves, that no payments are due for the use of the written music.

Library material

Is there *film* already in existence that suits your purposes? You might go to great trouble to record something that has already been filmed — in a way that suits your objectives and is better than you could make yourself. You might be able to use *part* of a film and improve on other parts, and/or edit unsuitable material out.

You may find that you need sequences that are extremely difficult or impossible to make yourself. Here are a few examples:

Part of a Nuremberg rally for a history programme.
Man walking on the moon — for a science programme.
Yaks in Nepal — for a geography programme.
Part of the Oberammagau passion play — for a religion programme.

Each of these would probably be impracticable – even in simulated form – for you to film yourself. Yet library film exists of each of them.

Film that has been taken by someone else is one of the great resources available to the producer, and can be a way of showing information that is impossible to show by other means. However, it should not be considered as a 'soft option' to taking film yourself – searching for film material can be a long, tedious, and frustrating business.

Ready-made film can come from a variety of sources. It is possible that your department already has a stock of film sequences, and that one of these will suit your purposes. If there is a news department, it is worth keeping in touch with it; a film of a bridge being built or of a local procession may be useful for an instructional programme when it is quite 'out of date' as far as the news people are concerned.

If you have not got them already, obtain copies of the catalogues of all the film libraries in your area. Besides commercial film libraries, embassies and large companies keep their own film libraries for loan to the general public for propaganda and information purposes. Universities are slowly building up libraries of film taken for research projects, though these may be hidden deep inside a department and can be difficult to unearth!

Unfortunately, film catalogues can give only a very general idea of the contents of a particular film. Probably you will have to spend many hours viewing large numbers of films with the possibility that, in the end, you will be unsuccessful. Film viewers that can run film at high speed – look for these in your editing department – can speed up the process enormously, but you still need to decide whether it is worthwhile committing your time – or that of an assistant – to this lengthy process.

Generally, the *maker* of a film has the right to say how it shall be used. When an organisation has paid someone to make the film, the organisation has this right. The person or organisation with this right is called the 'copyright holder'. Some copyright holders give permission very readily for their films to be used in other people's programmes. Some countries' information services take the view that it is part of their duty to get images of their country's achievements or characteristics onto the television screen, and, provided it is either obvious or is clearly stated which country is being shown, are happy to supply any amount of material.

Find out what kinds of film (16mm, 8mm, Super 8, etc) can be shown on your telecine machines. What running speeds can be used? This is rarely a problem with 16mm, but may be on 8mm or Super 8. What kinds of sound – optical, magnetic, separate magnetic – can be used?

If the film you wish to use is of a size or type that cannot be accepted by the telecine unit, you may have access to a laboratory that can copy it in a suitable form.

If the film cannot be used in telecine, nor can be copied, there is the rather drastic solution of using a television camera to shoot a screen image from a film projector.

Can the illumination on the television screen be made sufficiently even?

Is there a distracting 'flicker'?

Is there distracting distortion?

Your engineers will be able to help you attack these problems, but much depends on the characteristics of the particular projector and the particular television camera. If you need the sound from the film, ask the engineers if the projector can be connected directly to the studio circuitry, thus avoiding pick-up of sound in the studio. Whether or not you use the sound, you may find it convenient to videotape the sequence you want so as to use it as an insert in the programme.

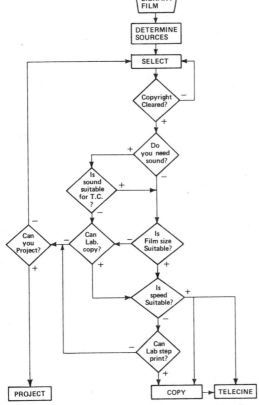

Decision sequence to determine use of library film.

Your own system is a source of recorded *videotape*. If you are remaking a programme, are there *parts* of the previous programme worth keeping? Are there parts of other programmes which would meet your requirements? What other stations use the same systems of video recording? If you orrow material from them, can it be used in your programmes?

If the problems of getting the borrowed recording onto your machines cannot be solved adequately, take a suitable playback machine to your studio and try pointing one of the studio cameras at the monitor. You will not get high quality this way, but you may get *adequate* quality. Put the monitor in a darkened area, and try to eliminate any reflections on the tube face. With some cameras the result may be that part of the picture produced by the camera is much brighter than the other part, the two parts being separated by a horizontal line. This is caused by the time relationship between th movement of the spot of light on the monitor screen and that of the beam in the camera tube. Pan the camera up and down until the dividing line disappears. It may help to tighten the shot and lose part of the picture, though picture quality will suffer, and you must be careful that vital picture information is not lost in the cut-off. From time to time a curved light line may pass across the picture. This is caused by lack of precision in the borrowed machine's pulses, but passes unnoticed in many scenes. You can record the camera's output on your own machines without any further difficulty, and recording the sound from one machine to another should be no problem.

Recorded sound may be teaching information in its own right. A history programme may need the recorded voice of a president declaring war, a music programme may need part of a symphony. The great difficulty is to find pictures that will not distract. It may be that the whole enterprise is better suited to radio. The usual compromise is to use graphics; a photograph of the president, a word caption for the symphony.

A well chosen *sound effect* may:

1. Give more realism to mute film.
2. Give atmosphere to drama.

An example of the first would be the roaring of lions to go with general pictures of lions in cages. However, if the particular lion shown does make a distinctive sound, it would be better to record it at the time of shooting.

As an example of the second, a small, room-like set in the studio may be made part of an airport, a railway station, or a hut in a storm in the jungle – simply by the choice of sound effects.

Many stations use background *music* without considering the purpose of it. The difficulties and dangers of using background music are:

1. Distraction.

   Music can drastically affect the 'mood' of a scene. In drama, this can be used to good effect – suppose you wish to change quickly from a scene at the Spanish Royal Court to the Inca palace of Atahualpa. Snatches of music will help to establish the change of scene. However, like all powerful tools, music must be used very carefully. Casual use of the first music record to come to hand may produce unwanted changes in the reactions of the audience. The music may have its own associations in the viewer's mind that have nothing to do with the content of the programme. Dance music can be particularly stimulating – pupils have been known to get out of their seats during a programme and start dancing around the classroom!

   There is music with no strong mood – such as the music used to make customers feel happier in a supermarket. Do you want to lull the senses when you are teaching?

2. Interference.

   Important teaching information may be contained in the sound of the programme. The obvious example is the spoken word, but other sounds in the programme may be important. If you are showing an antique clock, part of the stimulus for the viewer may be the slow deep-toned 'ticking' that it makes. This sound may be difficult to distinguish, or may be lost altogether, if background music is played at the same time.

It is a cliché to start a programme with credits and music. If you intend to use music in this way, time it, and look out for changes in mood and tempo. With skill and practice, you can synchronise the caption change with the music changes, but you must ask yourself if such time and effort could not be better expended in making the programme itself better. Precisely what are you *teaching* by all this? There is a considerable danger that this will take a great deal of production time and lead to neglect of more important matters. Credit music at the end of a programme can cause difficulties in the utilisation of the programme – if it is being used in a classroom in combination with a teacher, he will want to start working with the class the moment the programme ends, and a burst of music at this point will not help.

Just as with looking for any other pre-made material, searching for exactly the sound you want may be a long and frustrating business, and you should be open to the possibility of changing your mind and doing the recording yourself.

Radio studios and film dubbing theatres are good sources of recorded sound. Get in contact with any of these in your area, and try to obtain copies of their lists. In particular cases, there may be academic sources of the sounds you want – indigenous and/or aboriginal music may be on tape at the anthropological department of the university, for instance. You may find an agency to make up tapes of sound effects for you, and you can phone them and describe exactly what you need.

The performing rights for commercial records – those on sale in shops – are carefully guarded. Permission is needed from the makers for each use on television, and the fees may be high. The records used in radio stations and dubbing theatres may be subject to an agreement between the user and the manufacturer, whereby the records are used for a standard fee. Find out what payments have to be paid to use the material you want – the manufacturer or his agent will be able to tell you this if the station cannot. If copyright cannot be cleared economically, you must reject the record and start your search again.

Find out what kinds of recorded sound can be handled by the sound section of your television studio. You will probably have little difficulty in using any discs you have obtained. But audio tape comes in a great variety of track configurations and tape speeds, and you may have cassettes of a type that the studio cannot handle directly.

Material that is incompatible with the studio equipment must be copied into a form that *is* compatible, and the studio engineers should be able to help you with this. If you can find equipment that will play back the material you have, this can usually be connected to the studio equipment for copying.

If the equipment you have will play back the material but cannot be connected to the studio equipment, try holding a studio microphone close to, but not touching, the loudspeaker of this equipment, and record the result. You cannot get high quality this way, but the method can often produce intelligible results when all else fails.

Some of the sources of ready-made *photographs and drawings* are:

Graphic libraries – does your station have one?
Book libraries
Audio-visual centres
Museums
Information centres
Travel agencies
Embassies
Newspaper and magazine offices

Searching for ready made photographs and drawings can be a long and frustrating business with no guarantee that you will find what you want. Selection will depend on technical factors and on whether or not copyright clearance can be obtained. If there is difficulty with either, it may be better to use the information to help a graphics artist prepare what you want.

If you want to use a photograph or a drawing, find out who can give permission to use it. You may have to pay for the permission, but at this stage the important thing is to get the information – how much will it cost, how long will the formalities take before the final permission to use it.

In many fields, the 35mm still camera is used as a professional tool. Biologists use it to record flora and fauna in situ, geologists to record rock formations, architects to show places where they are going to build, and so on. The result is often a large collection of specialised *35mm colour slides*, and these can be a valuable source for your programme.

Slides should meet the following requirements:

1. The mount and aperture must be the right size for the telecine unit. For most telecine machines this is a 2 by 2 in mount with a 36mm x 24mm aperture. Most full size 35mm cameras produce this result. The Superslide which has a 40mm x 40mm picture in a 2 x 2 in mount, will also fill the screen, though much picture information will be lost at top and bottom.
2. Except in the case of the Superslide, the picture format should always be 'horizontal', i.e. 36mm *wide* by 24mm *high*. One that is only 24mm wide will not fill the television screen.
3. For black and white television, or colour television to be compatible with black and white receivers, no vital information must be conveyed by colour.
4. The 'safe area' must be adequate. A quite surprising amount of information is cut off by a telecine unit, even before allowance is made for cutoff at the receiver. Note, too, that the format of the slide is 3:2, which is much 'wider' than the television system's 4:3.
5. The essential information must be of sufficiently coarse detail to be resolved by the low definition system.
6. The composition must be adequate – it is no use asking telecine to 'zoom in a little' or 'pan right a bit'.

If your telecine is of the type that can change smoothly from one slide to another 'on air' you can present whole sequences entirely on telecine, thus freeing the studio to set up a new sequence.

If a slide does not meet the requirements for telecine, it may be possible to use it by copying it photographically to a form that you can use.

You can also try using a slide projector and screen in the studio, looking at the result with a studio camera. Do a test in the studio, and check the following:

a. If you are using front projection, you will be unable to avoid some distortion (unless you use the system called front axial projection). Is this distortion noticeable?
b. Is the illumination sufficiently even? This can be a big problem with rear projection.
c. Is the picture contrast adequate? Cut down all random light reaching the screen as far as possible.
d. Is picture definition adequate? The texture of the screen being used may be degrading the image.
e. Is the noise from the projector fan and its slide changing mechanism picked up by the studio microphones?

The advantages of this system are that, if a suitable projector is available, any size of slide can be used, and any selected part of the slide can be shown by framing the studio camera accordingly.

Two kinds of *filmstrips* are in common use:

Double frame

This has 36mm x 24mm pictures arranged horizontally along the length of the film.

Single frame

This has 24mm x 18mm pictures arranged vertically down the length of the film.

If you own a copy of a 35mm filmstrip in the double frame format, you can cut it up into individual frames and mount them in 2 x 2 in mounts and use them in telecine. Otherwise, use the techniques described above for slides not suitable for telecine.

Synthetics

Some equipment can produce a television image without needing an original 'subject'. The character generator – which produces an image direct from a keyboard – has already been mentioned. Find out what units are available in your system – they may provide a quicker and cheaper way of producing the image you want, though you should be careful to make sure that they meet the requirements for the transmitted image – definition, safe area, etc. – given by FASTDOTS.

Programme assembly

You need some kind of method of combining the sequence together, in order to form the complete programme.

Method 1. Assembly by TV control room

One method of preparing the programme is to arrange that everything takes place in a television studio. The cameras and microphones are placed and selected so as to give a clear presentation of what is happening. Picture and sound are sent to a videotape machine or directly transmitted. If the cables of the cameras and microphones are long enough, the programme action can take place outside the studio, still controlled from the studio control room. A television mobile unit has the control room inside a portable vehicle, but otherwise works in the same way, either recording the result on VTR machine in the vehicle or sending the signal to the 'parent' station by cable or microwave link.

A slightly more complicated procedure is to add telecine to the resources of the studio. Film sequences can then be included in the programme. A more complex arrangement also includes VTR playback machines, so that pre-recorded sequences can also be included.

Method 2. VTR assembly

Another method is to record each programme sequence separately, and then to 'edit' the resulting videotapes together to produce a complete programme. Not all videotape installations can do this, however. The subject is discussed in more detail under the heading VTR Editing. Film sequences are transferred to videotape before editing. The techniques for making VTR sequences for later assembly are basically the same as those for making complete programmes by Method 1, and for most of this book these techniques are described together – e.g. the direction of a television studio is the same whether a complete programme or just a sequence is being produced.

Method 3. Film production

The whole programme can be made on motion picture film, using cine cameras. For transmission the film is run through telecine. The basic techniques for making short sequences with simple equipment for inserting into television programmes made by other means are described in this book, but if you are to make complete programmes on film you should study the methods used by film makers. Such techniques are described, for example, in *The Technique of Documentary Film Production* by Hugh Baddeley, and *The Technique of Editing 16mm Film* by John Burder.

In addition to studying these techniques, you must remember that, as the result is to be shown on a *television* screen, you will also have to face the limitations of the television system. The most important of these are:

1. The *fine detail* that you can see when projecting your film onto a cinema screen will probably disappear when the film is transmitted by the low definition television system.
2. A colour television system (including the receiver) may not reliably produce the *colour* as you expect to see it, and a colour film of course loses all its colour if passed through a monochrome system or if reproduced by a monochrome receiver. The available contrast on the viewer's screen may also be very limited.
3. The amount of *picture area lost* by most telecine machines is quite remarkable, and the television receiver will then probably deduct its own percentage. The 'safe area' of the film frame is small – allow, say, 50% loss when planning where to put your teaching information.

Film for television, however, does have one important advantage over videotape – its compatability. If your film is made on 16mm stock with an optical sound track it can then be shown by virtually any television installation in the world – few television studios do not have access to a 16mm telecine, and the problems of line standards need not affect you in the slightest.

Decide programme format

The inputs to this stage are the evaluation information, the stylistic considerations, the programme strategies, which are all outputs of previous stages, and the resources available to make the programme.

Resources

You have already been keeping in mind the studio and other facilities available to make the programme. The other important variables are time, money and personnel.

Some large, sophisticated ETV systems give the producer a *comprehensive budget* and 'charge' him, at standard rates, for the use of the resources of the station. Personnel, studio time, film, and graphics all have standardised costs and the producer has to consider *all* his inputs in terms of his budget. Many kinds of trade-off are thus possible. If he has little need for graphics he can afford more studio time. Cutting down on the use of film may enable him to hire more or better actors, and so on. Even the 'fixed' station resources can be in-

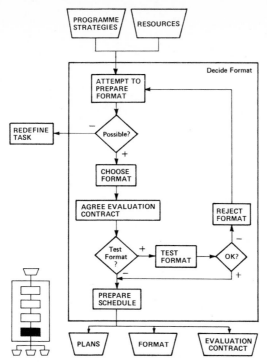

Determine format of programme.

creased by hiring resources from outside – the use of a bigger studio, of a sound-capable film team, a special high-speed film camera, etc.

Most stations, however, only give the producer a budget for what are called 'above the line' costs, that is expenditure above standard running costs. In too many stations the budget for above the line costs is in practice zero. This obviously biases the producer towards types of production that can be done in the TV studio in a routine way, even though more effective and even more economical (in terms of the total expenditure of the station) possibilities are, in fact, available.

How much *time* is there in which to make the programme?

How long is the programme?

Are there any limitations to the amount of studio time that can be used or the dates when it can be used?

Are there time limitations on the things you want for the programme such as library film only available after a certain date, holidays and other timetables of participants, etc.?

What *personnel* are available to work with the producer?

What are their special abilities?

What are their limitations?

Can other people be hired, if necessary?

Programme format

Write down the programme objectives. For each objective, write down sequences that will meet the objective, the station resources that you will use and the resources of time, money, and personnel that you will need.

Do the same for the method of assembly that you will use.

The result is a *programme format*.

Here is an example:

Objective	Sequence	Station	(Time) Prep	(Time) Prog	Resources (Money)	(Personnel)
To know where trees are found	Map with presenter	TV studio	30min	3min	nil	Scene hand
To recognise forest, types trees	Photos	Library	30min	2min	nil	Librarian
To identify tools used to cut tree	Borrowed saws (guest interview)	TV studio	2d	4min	fee $5?	Guest
To recognise technique of sawing	Film	Location film (mute)	3d	5min	$40?	Film cam team, dev. edit.
To experience tree crashing	Film fx.	as above lib. fx.	30min	2min	nil	Sound lib.
Total programme (assembly)	VTR	VTR, TV studio	2d	2min	below line	Studio team Telecine VTR Pres, Prod.
Totals			7d 2hr	18min	$45	
Available			10d	20min	$50	

You may be able to do this in a number of different ways.

If a series of programmes is to be made, and each programme has a similar set of objectives — as is the case with many series intended to cover part of a syllabus in a particular subject area, then it is possible to make a series of programme formats that contain similar elements.

For example, a teacher training series on new methods of teaching science in school might have *in each programme*:

1. An introduction by a presenter (TV studio)
2. Interview with teacher who tested the technique shown in the previous programme (TV studio)
3. Explanation of new technique by expert teacher (TV studio)
4. Excerpts from classroom using new technique (OB VTR)

5. Summary by presenter   (TV studio)
(Assembly: 1, 2, 3, 5 done as TV studio recording with 4 run in as pre-recorded VTR insert)

The objectives for each programme differ in detail, and so the actual sequences made will differ. However, each programme has the same kinds of sequence in the same order. This order is the *series format*.

When you have written the format, you can total the amount of facilities, time, money, and personnel that are needed.

There are now three possibilities:

A You have exactly the right number of sequences to fulfil the objectives, and the resources required are within those available.

B You have more than sufficient sequences to fulfil the objectives required, and can stay inside the limitations of resources and still fulfil the objectives.

C The programme cannot achieve the objectives without exceeding the resources available.

In Case A you now have a format, and can go on to the next stage, which is to agree the evaluation contract.

In Case B you have to choose a format from those available. Do this on a cost-effectiveness basis. Does one format imply a great deal of effort and programme time being expended on objectives that are not very important? Does another format offer simpler or shorter ways in which the objectives can be efficiently achieved? If the decision as to which format to use is a far-reaching one, it will be worthwhile to test some or all of the formats available.

Case C is quite common. The objectives cannot be met with the resources available. At this point, either the objectives must be reduced, or the resources increased. To do this you must report back to those who gave you the task in the first place. Do *not* proceed in the knowledge that the objectives required cannot be met.

Evaluation contract

The subject of evaluation is particularly confusing in television for education, which derives its concepts of evaluation from two sources – television and education. In commercial television, the basic evaluation is the calculation of audience 'ratings'. A programme's value is determined in terms of 'How many people watched?' and 'Did they like it?' A secondary evaluation is the weight given to the assessment of 'critics'. In education, the traditional evaluation system is based on a 'staircase' of examinations. Changes are taking place, however, and the growing emphasis on instructional objectives is changing evaluation systems.

An important change is that the traditional *norm-referenced* system of testing, which places students in a sequence of who is cleverer than who – who is 'first', 'second', etc. – is giving way to *criteria-referenced* testing which seeks to determine whether objectives are achieved. Obviously the result of the first is of little use to you as a producer, but the second tells you which parts of your programme were effective.

The concept of *accountability* is calling into question the effectiveness of educational systems and this has led to the evaluation of other elements of an educational system besides the students. It attempts to answer questions like, 'Which teaching methods are most effective?' and 'How *cost-effective* is the educational system?'

However evaluation is defined, fundamentally it is simply a process for measuring the value of something. If we look at this from a systems point of view than we can value three things – the outputs of the system, the inputs of the system, and the efficiency of the process of the system.

The emphasis in instructional television at the moment is mainly on output evaluation, and this takes many forms:

Critical assessment of programmes by a group of 'experts' who evaluate a programme in terms of how effective they think it will be on the basis of their professional experience. This method leaves the producer dependent on an 'opinion' as to what the programme ought to look like.

'Evaluation forms' returned by teachers which show whether the teachers liked the programme and thought it useful. This is probably the most widely used method. It reflects teachers' opinions of a programme as distinct from whether the programme achieved what it set out to do.

Estimates of *how many students* used a programme or a series. This may be linked to input costs to give a 'cost-benefit' evaluation.

Measurements of the extent to which the *objectives were achieved*. This is by far the most significant, provided that the tests actually measure what they are intended to measure (the tests are *valid*), and that they measure accurately and consistently (the tests are *reliable*).

Many producers become nervous of the evaluation process. It may seem, and may be, arbitrary and unrelated to what the producer is trying to do. To avoid this, and to make sure that the evaluation is fair and useful, begin a dialogue with the evaluator when you are identifying outputs and inputs. Agree your objectives with the evaluator, otherwise he will not be measuring what you are intending to achieve and vice versa. If there is a big gulf between what you think you are trying to do and what he thinks you should be trying to do, perhaps you should both discuss this with whoever is responsible for the overall project.

Do not expect this to be simple, or to be resolved by written statements. You are trying to form a strategy for the programme by relating a large number of variables, and it is a dynamic situation. However, before any ouput evaluation takes place, you should enter into a 'contract' with the evaluator, in which you are saying,

'Given this defined audience, this defined context, and these defined resources, I expect the programme to achieve x% of its objectives with y% of the audience, and I understand that it will be evaluated on this basis.'

If you can establish such an agreement with your evaluator, you will eliminate much of the confusion that can exist in evaluation, and the results of the evaluation will be useful to you.

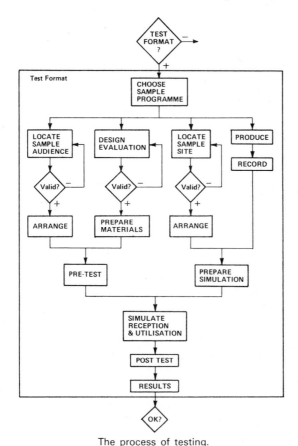

The process of testing.

Testing is expensive. However, if you are involved in an expensive series aimed at a large audience, it is essential to make sure that you have a good format before launching into full production. This involves making a programme – a 'typical' programme if you are testing a series format – and measuring its effect on a sample audience. The full process is shown in the diagram on page 91.

This is a long, complicated and expensive process. However, most of it is the task of the evaluator. Your task is to make the (sample) programme. To do this, use the techniques described in the rest of this book. The results of the evaluation will tell you where the programme was most and where least effective. This enables you to make decisions about future production.

Prepare plan of production

As a result of the processes so far described in the book, you should now be able to set down the following for your programme:

The objectives of the programme
The audience for the programme
The context of the programme
How long the programme(s) will be
Resources required for the programme
List of people selected
List of things to be made
List of things to be obtained
List of graphics to be made
List of graphics to be obtained
List of film to be made
List of film to be borrowed
List of film editing or processing to be done
List of sound to be pre-recorded
List of sound to be borrowed
List of VTR sequences to be recorded
List of VTR sequences to be obtained
Copyright data.

These will be inputs for the subsystems of the preparation system.

Production schedule

To decide whether the production as now planned is feasible, you need to make a *production schedule*.

Planning for television production is usually dominated by the concept of 'deadline'. Suppose a specially shot film sequence is to be used in a programme on a particular day – call it day X. It must be edited, at the latest, the day before, day $X - 1$. Suppose processing takes three days. Then filming cannot take place after day $X - 5$ or it will be impossible to have it processed and edited in time. The deadline for the filming is day $X - 5$.

Factors of station organisation may also be involved. In the above case, suppose that the film crew will be away on another assignment from $X - 10$ to $X - 7$. Then filming for your programme must either be done before $X - 10$ or on $X - 6$ or $X - 5$. But you want to use $X - 6$ for auditioning, so that ... (and so on). Planning the production schedule thus becomes a sort of jig-saw puzzle. An example of such a schedule is given below.

The whole thing becomes more complicated when various activities interact — some graphics will be used in the pre-filming, or a graphic is a diagram which will be based on a scene from the film. The various deadlines then become interdependent. In really complicated productions, management techniques may be used to plan the interrelationships of the activities.

	X-11	X-10	X-9	X-8	X-7	X-6	X-5	X-4	X-3	X-2	Dry Run X-1	Recording
LIBRARY FILM		View		Send lab.	MIN. PERIOD			Collect Lab.	Edit	Pre Dub		
SPECIAL FILM	Recce.		Shoot	Send lab.	MIN. PERIOD			Collect Lab.	Edit			
GRAPHICS							Order	MIN. PERIOD		Collect		
SCRIPT											Write final	
FLOOR PLAN						Prepare						
PEOPLE					Audition							
SCENERY							Order					

Example of production schedule.

Is the schedule feasible?

Perhaps it is. However, deadlines may turn out to be incompatible, or equipment that was originally expected to be available is out of action. The investigations you have carried out may show that there are unforeseen difficulties in doing the programme the way that was originally planned. In all these cases there is no alternative but to replan, making modifications until the schedule is feasible.

Submission of programme plan

The acceptance of a production plan may involve different groups of

93

people, each with different interests. These groups may include:

Station management – does it approve the format and the expenditure?

Ministry of Education – does it approve the basic project?

Teachers' representatives – do they approve the objectives?

If the plan is accepted first time, you are lucky. At some stations, the plans are returned several times for modifications.

6 Preparation system

We now come to the preparation stage. This is shown below in the context of the production system.

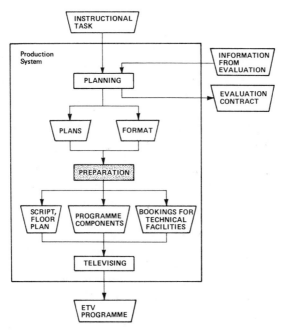

The production system: a simplified version of the key (see page 17). Locating the preparation stage.

Below is the preparation system. For the subsystem "Obtain components" we shall look separately at Obtain people, Obtain things, Obtain graphics, Library film.

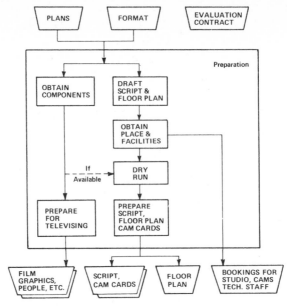

The preparation system.

Obtain people

The process to obtain people is shown on page 97. The input is the list of participants from the plan of production, page 92.

Both the vocabulary and the speech speed of participants must be suitable for the audience. Even a competent teacher may need reminding of the actual audience when he is faced with nothing but cameras and microphones. Guests and demonstrators may have greater difficulty.

Will the words that the participant speaks be written down beforehand? Again, for some people, writing the words down results in a stilted presentation, when the same person can 'ad lib' most effectively. For some other people the reverse is the case. Some people can read fluently from a script card held in front of the camera (a 'jumbo card') or a 'teleprompter', but this is much more difficult than it appears, and, before committing yourself to it, you need to be convinced that the participant is really capable of using this technique.

A well worded *contract* may save you a great deal of trouble later on. Will the participant be paid? When will he be paid? Will he be paid again if the programme is repeated? When and where will he have to attend? What preparation work will he need to do? Will he be reimbursed for expenses that he incurs?

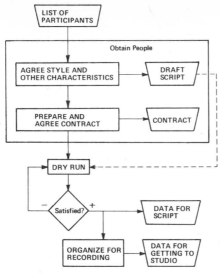

Preparing people for the studio.

Obtain things

As you obtain each object for the programme, following your plan of production, examine each object critically in terms of its use in the television studio. Commercially made models, in particular, are often bright and shiny, giving dazzling reflections of studio lights. Your graphics department may be able to spray down offending bright surfaces with 'anti-flare' – or, in emergency, hair lacquer, or may even sandpaper surfaces to a matt finish or repaint them. Repainting may also be necessary if the details cannot be seen by the television camera for lack of adequate contrast. If in doubt, check each item with the cameras that you will use for the programme.

When you are in the position of commissioning objects to be made, you can include the above requirements in your original order, together with the other requirements of objects for television.

When you prepare a *demonstration* don't forget that it will have to be carried out several times. In a studio, cameramen and lighting engineers need to see the demonstration before the programme is recorded. A common, but most unwise, practice, is to 'mime' the demonstration during rehearsals, saving the actual materials until the recording. The recording may, however, have to be repeated. Some special difficulty such as an unexpected reflection or shadow, or one part of the demonstration obscuring some other part, will then not be seen until it is too late to rectify it. Murphy's First Law applies par-

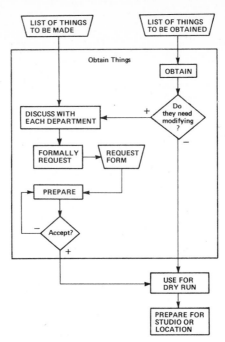

| LIST OF THINGS TO BE MADE | | LIST OF THINGS TO BE OBTAINED |

Obtain Things

OBTAIN

DISCUSS WITH EACH DEPARTMENT + Do they need modifying ?

FORMALLY REQUEST → REQUEST FORM

PREPARE

Accept?

USE FOR DRY RUN

PREPARE FOR STUDIO OR LOCATION

Preparing things for the studio.

ticularly to television – 'If anything *can* go wrong, it will.' Arrange for sufficient consumables to be available for at least half a dozen performances of the demonstration in the studio. You should do the same if the demonstration is to be filmed, particularly if crucial parts of the demonstration are to be filmed in long shot *and* in close-up.

If you are using live plants, insects, reptiles, or other animals, you will need to make special arrangements to keep them alive! When will they arrive? Who will look after them and feed and/or water them? Where will they be kept before they go into the studio? Plants, like animals and children, wilt under studio lights. Reptiles, however, come 'alive'. A studio once emptied rapidly when a previously sleepy cobra became very lively during a recording.

Obtain graphics

Explaining precisely what you want to the people who will make your graphics materials is a difficult process. Prepare storyboards and/or graphics request forms. Be as specific as possible, but remember that the people who work in these departments have artistic skills and abilities and can make suggestions that may improve your programme. Discuss your storyboard with them and be prepared to

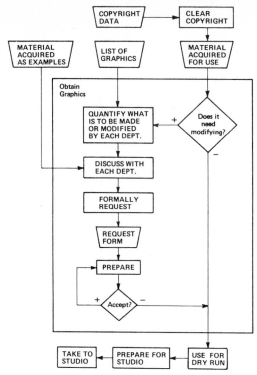

Preparing graphics to the studio.

modify it. Give the artist relative information about the audience and the message and ask him to design the graphic.

The artist may present you with 'thumb nail' rough sketches. You must then decide if the presentation is what you want. If it is not, then explain further to the artist, so that he can try again. While the material is being prepared it may be a good idea to call in to see the artist once or twice to make sure that your storyboard is understood and that the artist is doing what you want and is keeping on schedule.

You may be needed in the preparation of any *still photographs*. If you want stills taken of a particular object or a 'photo story', then the photographer will want you to be present and direct the taking of the photographs.

Library film

If a *sequence of film* is suitable for telecine, but you wish to re-edit it, you will need to have a copy. *Never* cut a borrowed film. Libraries

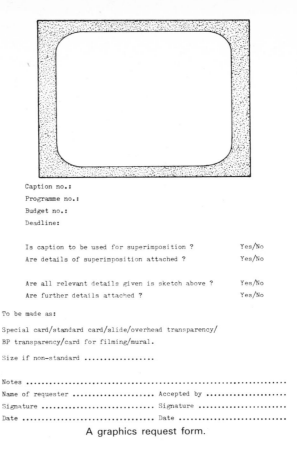

Caption no.:
Programme no.:
Budget no.:
Deadline:

Is caption to be used for superimposition ?   Yes/No
Are details of superimposition attached ?   Yes/No

Are all relevant details given is sketch above ?   Yes/No
Are further details attached ?   Yes/No

To be made as:

Special card/standard card/slide/overhead transparency/
BP transparency/card for filming/mural.

Size if non-standard ....

Notes ....
Name of requester .... Accepted by ....
Signature .... Signature ....
Date .... Date ....

A graphics request form.

are, quite understandably, very sensitive on this subject. A film that is unsuitable for telecine will also have to be copied.

Once you have your own copy, you can edit and dub this just as if it were film you had shot yourself.

The highest quality copy is that made from the original negative — or, in the case of a colour film, the colour master. In the production process of a major film, the next stage is the 'fine grain' or the 'inter-negative', and good copies can be made from these. If you can borrow any of these, your laboratory can make one or more high quality copies that you can then edit as you like. If you are offered a choice, consult with the laboratory as to which they would prefer. Both 'fine grains' and 'internegatives' are very easily damaged and may be irreplaceable. Unless you are quite confident that you know how to prepare these for the laboratory, take the film can(s) along to the laboratory *unopened*, and ask them to show you. The laboratory may ask you whether you want DIN or SMPTE prints. The difference is not important unless you are going to edit the result with other film from different sources. If you are, discuss this with the laboratory so that you get the kind of print you need. It is quite likely that the only copy available to you to copy from will be the print in the film library. Copies *can* be made from this, but the quality will be lower, and any damage or dirt on the copy will be faithfully reproduced on your copy.

Take a projector and the film along to the dry run, so that the cast can see the film and understand how it fits into the programme. This also applies to film that you are going to use in the studio with a projector. *Durations* of all film sequences and how they are going to be shown should be noted for putting in the script.

Copies that you have had made can be assembled into the reel with the other telecine sequences you have made, but library film that you are going to use without having had it copied needs rather different preparation.

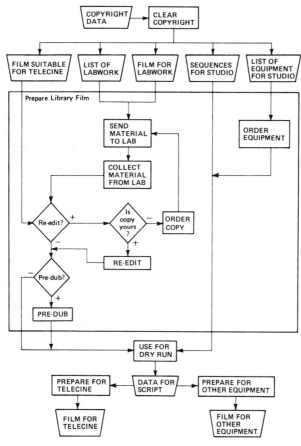

Preparing library film for the studio.

Draft script and floor plan

While the various elements are being prepared, you can draft a script and a floor plan. The detail in which these can be prepared depends on the degree of predictability of the programme. In this book we shall discuss three categories of programme.

1. *Fully planned and predictable*
   In this case you know in advance what every movement will be, and every word that will be spoken. You can plan precisely what shots will be used, and the exact moment when you will use them. Examples include: an expert teacher with demonstrations of equipment that he knows well; most kinds of drama; programmes using film and captions.

2. *Planned but with unpredictable elements*
   In a sequence that is a discussion between two or more people, you can plan what shots to use, but (provided the discussion is a real one, and not a drama in disguise) you cannot predict in advance the precise moments when you will use each shot, nor can you predict the exact words that will be used. If you use animals or children in your programme, you may be able to plan where abouts they will be during the programme, and at what point in the programme you will use them, but their exact movements will be unpredictable.

   A 'topical' programme may have to change its content at the last moment, perhaps even while the programme is being transmitted 'live'. A news programme, or a daily programme about the weather are both examples of this.

3. *Unpredictable*
   If you need to show *behaviour*, whether of people or of animals, the precise content will be unpredictable. To show aspects of child psychology or group dynamics, it is important that the behaviour be 'real' and not altered for television. You set up a particular situation and *observe* it with the television equipment. It is usually necessary to record a lot of activity and then edit it to show the required points in a reasonable time.

   These three cases require different methods of control. We shall classify them as follows:

Material		*Method*
Planned & predictable	→	Systematic direction
Planned but unpredictable	→	'Emergency' direction
Unpredictable	→	Observation techniques

Planned and predictable – systematic direction

With everything under your control, you can draft a script and a floor plan. Both of these are based on the kind of shots you need. A systematic approach to deciding this is in Appendix I. A guide as to how to draw a floor plan is in Appendix II.

There are many ways in which a *script* can be laid out – unless there are serious objections to this, use the layout that is commonly used by your system. A script for systematic direction should show:

The source of each shot – be it a camera, telecine, VTR, generator, or a combination of two or more of these.
A brief description of the shot.
Details of the sound – source and content.
How the moment of transition from one shot to another is determined – by a word cue, by a duration or by a movement.

A specimen script made to one suitable layout is shown below. Notice the 'shot numbers' in the left hand column – these are essential for systematic direction.

Planned but unpredictable – 'emergency' direction

If you have invited a guest for an interview you cannot predict what he is going to say, word for word. Animals in the studio are notoriously unpredictable in their movements. In such cases, you need a 'cover shot' – one camera taking a general view of the area, perhaps – a shot that you can cut to 'whatever happens'. You cannot write down the transitions precisely, and you will have to give sudden orders in the control room during the recording. The script for such a section would look like this. Be careful not to get trapped without a cover shot in this kind of sequence – if all the cameras are taking close-ups in a sequence there might well be a moment when none is giving an acceptable shot.

Specimen operational script

| 8 | 1 and 2 intercut as directed | 1: 2–S Betty and animal | Betty – "We don't often have animals . . . . " |
| | | 2: CU animal | to "So, last Saturday, I went along to see the new zoo at St. Helen's." |

The floor plan is worked out in the same way as for systematic direction.

103

Specimen Operational Script
(Butterfly sequence)

21.	1.	2–S Presenter and Butterfly	Not all insects are as ugly as the elephant beetle – some of them are astonishingly beautiful.
22.	2.	CU Butterfly	This is the Lavender Hill butterfly, which is usually found on the slopes of Mount Zurabozo. If you have been therein July or August you will have seen great clouds of butterflies just like this one. I want you to look very carefully at this one's head.
23.	1.	BCU Head (in Proj. microscope)	Now it doesn't look so beautiful – does it! Do you remember what those things sticking out from its head are called? (PAUSE)
24.	SUPER 1 and CG. MIX	1. BCU Head CG: "ANTENNAE"	They are called antennae. Now we will see them being used.
25.	Telecine (2 next)	Seq. 3: Butterfly (Dur: 3' 43″)	GRAMS: Disc OXY 135 A3 Forest fx. Hold under.

Unpredictable – observation techniques

You cannot push a large studio camera into a group and expect the group to behave normally. You may be able to get near enough with a small, hand-held camera, particularly if it is not trailing a cable. This implies that the cameraman or his assistant is carrying the VTR unit. How do you communicate with the cameraman in this situation? Is it feasible to be the cameraman yourself? A technique which often works surprisingly well is to use a large mobile camera with a powerful zoom lens. Divide the floor area – whether it is the studio or not – into two areas, one for the activity, and the other for the camera to move freely. Lighting can be fairly simple, consisting of sufficient light from behind the camera area to illuminate the activity area. Microphones should be suspended over likely movement areas. A boom is impractical and distracting, and neck microphones even more so, but superdirectional microphones can be tried if you have them available.

Determine exactly what phenomena you are looking for. What is it you hope to see? Make a list of the kinds of shots you want. Is there any sequence to what you will see? Will the kinds of shots change? What might happen?

The result might look something like this – an example from a programme on group dynamics with eight year old children:

Specimen operational script
(Group dynamics)

1. Group – children round sand tray.
   (They may form a little group a little distance from the tray, or might even move away from it)

   Voices of group – individual detail not needed.

2. Individual shots of children to observe manifestations of leadership, support for leadership, opposition to leadership or any child who avoids participation in group activities. Relationships between children more important than close-ups.

   Need to pick up individual voices clearly.
   Some may move around. Some may *whisper*.

Obtain place and facilities

If possible, hold a 'planning meeting' a week or so before the day of the recording. The designer and the senior engineer assigned to the programme should attend, and the presence of the lighting engineer (if different) and the floor manager will be helpful. Take along your tentative floor plan and a script or running order, so that you can discuss in detail the content of the programme and the organisation of facilities. As a result of the meeting, book the studio and/or facilities and the designer can start work on the scenery. The designer or you yourself should now make an exact floor plan.

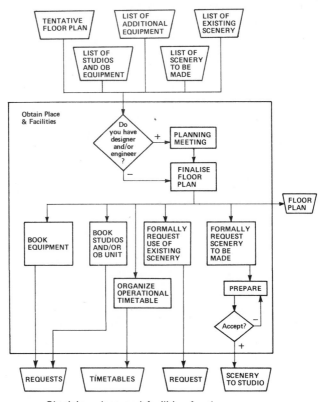

Obtaining place and facilities for the programme.

Dry run

For 'systematic' and 'emergency' direction, arrange a day when all the *participants* – not the studio crew – can meet together with you to rehearse the programme.

This is, of course, a technique much used by the theatre, and many of the same methods can be used. You will need a sufficiently large room, all the properties and demonstrations that are going to be used in the programme, and preferably all the captions and other visuals. Set everything up in the room as near as you can to your studio floor

106

plan, putting marks on the floor to simulate the positions of scenery and technical equipment. Go carefully through the programme as many times as are necessary to make sure that everybody knows exactly what he will be required to do. The ideal is to be able to spend all your studio time on technical problems, and to be able to take the 'content' for granted. What the educational television director must avoid is using the studio for purposes which could perfectly well have been completed beforehand, while the studio crew stands about idle.

For unpredictable ('observation techniques') direction, the last thing you want to do is rehearse. However, the more you know of the likely behaviour, the better. Does a similar situation exist which you can observe beforehand? If it is a demonstration of children's behaviour in a certain situation, can you see what another group of children do in the same situation?

Prepare script and camera cards

You should prepare the *floor plan* (final version). You may have to make do with just the original, but it is very useful to have several copies.

You need to prepare the *script*, with as many copies as there are people in the studio crew, plus participants, plus as many again for safety – scripts disappear in a mysterious way in television studios! It is an advantage if they are not printed on white paper.

You also need to prepare *camera cards* from the script, one card for each cameraman (and one for his assistant, if he has one). A specimen camera card is shown below.

Specimen camera card
(butterfly sequence)

CAMERA			Card 2 of 2
21	A	2–S	Presenter and butterfly
23	A	BCU	Head (in projection microscope)
26	A	CU	Presenter

Prepare for televising

Particularly if it is the participant's first appearance on television, make sure that he knows exactly *when* and *where* to come for the recording. It is a good idea to have exact information typed out and given to him. Include a telephone number at which you can be reached in an emergency and get one through which you can get in touch with him.

Graphics

At the earliest opportunity after you receive the captions, check them through carefully. Your check should include the following:

1. Is the teaching information correct? It is amazing how teaching errors can creep in. In particular make quite sure that any words or numbers used are correct.
2. Is all information inside the safe area?
3. Is contrast adequate? If in doubt, test the graphic with a camera and a low quality monitor.
4. Do the animations operate smoothly? Do you know how they work?
5. Can the information be shown easily on a 4:3 screen? Is size adequate for the pans and zooms needed?
6. Have the superimpositions been made white on black?

Once you have received and approved them, label all the captions and slides, firstly by their shot number (taken from the script), and secondly by the name of the video source that will show them (camera 1, camera 2, telecine, caption scanner, etc.). Place them in groups according to their 'source' and put them in sequence so that when you enter the studio you can distribute them quickly, easily, and accurately.

Pre-recorded sound

If your plan is to use the various sound contributions separately – i.e. no two sources are ever used together – it is preferable to transfer all your material to tape. Under the intense working conditions of a television studio, discs can get scratched, dirtied, or even dropped, and thus made unusable. Tape, on the other hand, although not entirely foolproof, is far less vulnerable. Even if you do damage it, you can make another transfer from the original material. It makes life much easier, too, to assemble the various bits of tape in the order in which you are going to use them. If a section is to be used twice, make two transfers, and splice them into the new tape in order. An operator moving steadily from one tape section to the next is obviously less likely to make mistakes than one desperately trying to rewind and find a section while the programme is running. Separate sections by lengths of coloured tape, and list all the sections, in order, for your script.

If you are going to mix recordings, and no more than two sources are to be played at a time, you can use two tape recorders and assemble two sets of tape. The final mixing is then done while the programme is being recorded. With two tape recorders and a disc player you can mix a disc with a tape and record the result. A friendly radio station can help you with the techniques required. Synchronising 'spot' sounds — hammers, locomotive puffs, and so on — with screen action is very difficult in the TV system, and if you need this you will probably be better off with a film dubbing studio and expert operators.

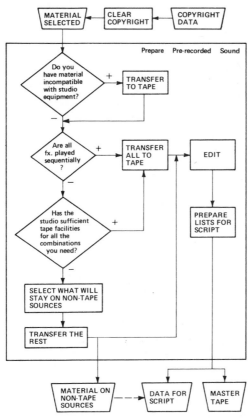

Preparing pre-recorded sound.

Library still pictures

Most of the graphics you find will not have been made specifically for television. They may have serious deficiencies which need correction.

You cannot expect all graphics to be the *shape* of the television screen (about four units wide by three high, though some receivers have screens that are five units by four high). Is it possible to select a part that is this shape, and still show all the information needed? Could you pan or tilt from one part to another? Can the picture be cut out and mounted on a piece of card that *is* in the correct format?

Can the necessary *detail* be seen on the screen when the whole graphic is shown? Can the studio cameras show part of the graphic so that the required detail becomes visible? Can you rephotograph the graphic and enlarge the required part?

The picture seen by the viewer is less than the *area* that the camera sees, and moreover it is awkward and time consuming for a cameraman to have to line up exactly on the edges of a graphic. If important information is on the edge of the graphic you need to find some way of reframing it, perhaps by cutting out some objects with scissors and pasting them on to a more central part of the graphic.

Studio graphics are made in *standard sizes*. While it is possible for a studio camera to frame captions of different sizes, this can be a nuisance if you need to show a series of pictures. You can overcome this by having the pictures rephotographed and then either printed to the standard size or made into slides for use in telecine.

Glossy pictures can be used in the studio – you need to mount the picture on a flat, rigid surface, and then light it obliquely so that no reflections go into the camera lens – but it may be more convenient to rephotograph the picture and print onto a matt surface.

If you have been given a copy of the picture with *distracting* or redundant information, or can rephotograph it, you can cut out the essential information and mount it on a plain background. An alternative is to shade out unwanted information with pencil or ink.

Library film for telecine

The telecine operator needs to know exactly where in the film each sequence that you are going to use starts. If you prepare the film carefully in advance you can save him a lot of trouble and save yourself unnecessary delays.

First, mark the beginning of the sequence that you want to use, with a wax pencil. Mark with a large cross the frame before the start of the sequence. You can make this more noticeable by drawing lines to the cross from a short length before it (not after, or the lines will appear on the screen).

When the telecine operator finds this section, he can lace the machine so that the marked frame is in the gate. When the machine is run, the required sequence will appear on the screen.

In this photograph the vehicle is shown clearly, but the background is distracting.

Here the part of the photograph that is the vehicle is cut out and pasted on to a neutral background.

The wax mark now shows where the required sequence starts. However, it is tedious for the telecine operator to have to wind slowly through a thousand feet or more of film looking for a wax mark, so you can help him by adding some more obvious identifications. Get some brightly coloured opaque adhesive tape and stick a small patch of this on the film just before the wax marks, taking care not to cover any sprocket holes. This will be much easier for him to spot as the film goes through a rewinder. A further technique that makes life much easier for the operator is to insert a small piece of paper in between the successive layers of film on the reel at about the position of the sequence. For a sequence contained in a long film it is useful to use all three techniques.

After the programme has been recorded, don't forget to remove all these marks − the wax marks will polish off with a handkerchief, and

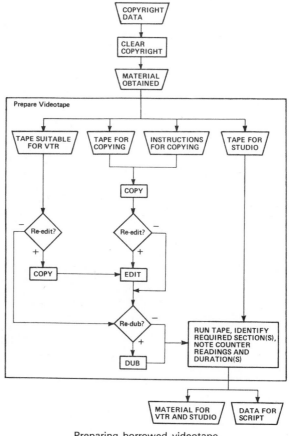

Preparing borrowed videotape.

any marks left by the tape can be removed with a cloth soaked in carbon tetrachloride. Get somebody in the film department to show you the difference between the 'base' and 'emulsion' sides of the film and always put the wax marks on the 'base' side, so that they will clean off easily.

If you have a very good VTR installation at your disposal, you can bypass all this by simply recording the film material you want to use – perhaps using library prints if they are in good condition – and doing your editing using the VTR equipment.

Borrowed videotape

If you have suitable equipment, you can edit the sequences by copying them onto videotape, and you can, if you wish, change the sound on the copy, though it is usually simpler to run the tape 'mute' as part of your programme and add the sound from the studio. In all cases you need to measure and note the duration of each sequence you are going to use. Any borrowed tape should, of course, be carefully identified and kept physically separate from your own recordings.

7 Production system

The following sections of this book are for the person who controls the television situation – be it studio, long cable, or mobile unit – directing the cameraman and the rest of the operational staff in order to record or transmit the required programme. In some stations this work is done by the programme producer, others have a separate 'director'.

If the producer and director are separate, the producer should not consider himself part of the studio team but should be present during the televising processes. He should not interfere directly with the technical details or the activities taking place. It is irritating and frustrating for a director to have a producer who is a 'back seat driver' and errors in communication can easily take place. The producer should sit in the control area and *watch and listen.* Any criticism or suggestion should be noted on a copy of the script and discussed with the director at a suitable break.

Whether or not the producer and director are the same person, an assistant director can be most useful, and can make a great difference to the smooth running of a complicated programme. The director can stay in charge and avoid leaving the control area on petty errands. If a graphic needs an adjustment and the graphics department doesn't answer the 'phone, or if Professor Grump has been seen heading for the bar instead of the make-up room, the assistant director can be sent to resolve the problem.

Staff

To do your programme direction in a systematic way, you will need the following personnel:

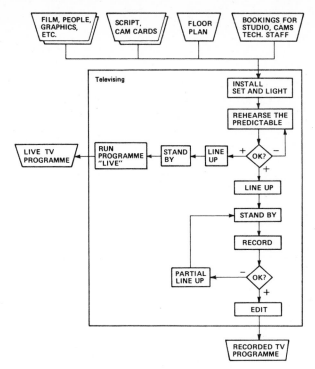

The televising system.

Vision mixer
Director's assistant (*not* the assistant director)
Floor manager
plus the usual studio crew – say cameramen, microphone operator(s) lighting engineer, video operator, audio mixer. If you have film inserts you may need a telecine operator, and if you have VTR inserts, a VTR operator, though in some big stations neither of these is part of the *studio* team, and the signals are sent from an installation some distance from the studio itself. If you are going to record the programme, you will need a VTR operator, whether or not the VTR is part of the studio.

The requirements for emergency direction are similar, though the director's assistant will have much less to do, and some directors prefer to do their own vision mixing.

Observation techniques will need a vision mixer only if more than one camera is used. A good director's assistant can take notes during the recording that will save a great deal of time at the editing stage. The floor manager will probably have little to do, but is useful for emergencies.

115

Install, set and light

Have the scenery and properties installed in the studio in accordance with your floor plan. In a well organised station with an efficient floor manager, all this is done for you, but you should be present during this stage in case you have made any mistakes in your plan.

Allow time for the lighting to be set up. The time needed for this depends on the complexity of your plan and the particular kind of lighting supports installed. Some stations have motorised poles to support the lights which can be moved quickly along battens that are themselves mobile. With such equipment even complicated arrangements can be set up quickly. Another studio, where everything has to be done with ladders and spanners, may need far more time for even a much simpler set up. A good clear floor plan makes it possible for the lighting engineers to start work early, even before the scenery has been brought in.

If you are working with a *mobile unit*, you may have to do some rearranging of your floor plan. If you are installing lights, check where the *reflections* are, these can have a disastrous effect during the recording, so cover up, reangle or remove glass doors; glass covered pictures, chrome surfaces.

Rehearse the predictable systematic direction – looking at shots

The way you arrange the seating in the control room will probably depend on the fixed positions of the equipment. The vision mixer, obviously, will need to be at the vision mixing unit, which is almost certainly immovable. Seat yourself at his side, the side where there is more room. If the microphone to the cameraman is fixed to the desk you must be within reach of it and so must your assistant, who sits on your other side. In some control rooms the sound mixer is also in the same room, with his turntables, disc units, and the mixing panel. In other arrangements there is a separate sound control room.

Establish your *communication* with the cameramen and with your floor manager. For some reason this is often a delaying and frustrating business in many studios. You may have to go on to the studio floor and ask the cameramen and the floor manager to put on their headsets, or you may be able to do this from the control room by means of 'loudspeaker talkback'. In a few well organised stations the staff will have their headsets on and be ready to go at the scheduled time of rehearsal. There are three possible ways in which cameraman may communicate with you:

116

1. Their headsets may contain a microphone and when they speak you can hear them, either through your own headset or through a small loudspeaker on the control desk.
2. They may use a microphone already on the floor for the production, and speak through that. You will then hear their voices through the 'programme sound' loudspeaker. Some sound mixers put an omnidirectional microphone in the studio purely for talkback purposes, and fade it out for the recording.
3. They may use simple signals by *moving the camera*. Swinging it rapidly from side to side – moving the image on the monitor from side to side – is used to mean 'No' and panning it up and down – producing vertical movements of the image – means 'Yes'.

The floor manager generally has to use the second method unless he has been supplied with a special microphone. Otherwise he can move in front of one of the cameras and give signals – hopefully polite ones – visually. The first two methods are useless during recording, as voices in the studio are liable to be picked up by the microphones and recorded.

Once communication has been established, tell the floor manager that you are going to '*look at shots*' and ask him to have the actors, etc. ready.

Ask each cameraman in turn to give the shot marked on his camera card. Ask the vision mixer to select the shot (this is so that it appears on the monitors on the studio floor). Examine the shot carefully. Does it show precisely what is needed? Does it meet the FASTDOTS requirements?

If the answers to any of these questions are unsatisfactory, have the shot changed, either by changes to the subject or to the way the studio is showing it. This is a crucial point in the development of the programme, so worry away at the shot until it is as good as you can make it. Then tell the cameraman 'That's it – that is your shot no. '

The cameraman should then make a note of exactly where the camera is – possibly by marking the floor with wax crayon and noting the camera height – and should write on his camera card whatever information he needs so that he can exactly repeat the shot whenever required. Such information might include the lens being used and a note of what objects are in shot, for example. The floor manager should also make marks so that he can be sure that the performers, the scenery, and the properties will be in exactly the same places the next time the shot is needed.

Repeat this process for each succeeding shot, until each shot in the programme has been discussed and the details noted. At this stage this does not include film or VTR inserts, and it is a matter of choice whether or not to include slides and captions, unless the latter involve camera moves.

A similar briefing may now take place for the audio mixer.

The vision mixer will need to know at what precise moments he must change from each shot to the next. In many types of programme this is obvious as it depends on a particular word being spoken, as marked in the script. Other changes may be signalled by a visual cue – when a particular object is touched, for example, or, especially in the case of film sequences, on a particular timing. Go through the script with the vision mixer, explaining the moment for each change. He should then mark his script clearly with these changes so that he can read his script quickly and accurately in the (often low level) lighting in the control room.

Stagger through

This is the first attempt to present the complete programme. The members of the team attempt to run the programme by reference to their own notes. The vision mixer selects each shot in turn by following his script and the action on the monitor screens. He chooses the exact moment to make each transition by reference to the notes that you gave him during the previous stage. In the same way the audio operator keeps his operations 'in step' with the programme. As each shot appears, the director's assistant calls out the shot number of *the shot that is on the screen*. Notice that he is not giving orders – he is calling out the actual 'position' of the programme. Everybody else uses these numbers as their guide as to when to carry out the operations that have already been agreed. A cameraman, for example, who has shots 15 and 18 on his camera card, has discussed and agreed the content of both these shots with the director in the previous phase. While he is 'offering' shot 15, he sees his tally light come on, and hears the director's assistant say 'Shot 15'. A little later he sees the light go off, and hears 'Shot 16'. Without waiting for any further instruction, he moves his camera into position for his next shot – shot 18. He hears shot 17 called, and by this time is ready with his next shot. As his tally light comes on he hears 'Shot 18'. And so on.

There will be initial mistakes and problems. These may be due to operators misunderstanding their original instructions, mistakes or inadvertent changes by the speaker, or to your initial instructions being impossible.

Examples of the latter are when the position of one camera for a particular shot puts it in the field of view of the previous camera, when there is sufficient time for a camera move, and so on. In the 'stagger through' it is essential to *stop* immediately and sort out the

118

problem. Remember, if you do not stop, the problem merely persists until the next stage.

Once stopped, sort the problem out. You may well be able to do this from the control room, by asking for a position to be changed, delaying a cut, and so on. On many occasions the solution will be obvious to those on the floor ('go round the back') and can be sorted out quickly by them. More complicated difficulties may require you to go onto the studio floor to sort them out, though this is relatively time consuming. Be prepared to listen to the suggestions of the people on the floor – they may have a better view of what precisely is causing the problem, and from their own experience may be able to suggest a quick solution. Remember, though, that the ultimate responsibility remains yours. For any programme there are a number of good ways of doing it, and possibly more than one excellent way. You are the one who has to choose between the various possibilities. The team may make suggestions, but you make the decisions.

Notice that we have *not* suggested that the director gives orders while the programme is going on. As we have already noted, the director is one of the few, if not the only person, who knows precisely what the completed programme should be like. It is essential that he should be able to watch and listen to the programme. A mistake that slips past him is unlikely to be corrected by anybody else. We suggest that he concentrates on this role during this and the following stages. When anything fails to work properly, he should call 'stop', and *then* – only then – start to give orders.

In order to give more time to the 'looking at shots' and 'stagger through' stages of production, it is generally convenient, for a complicated programme, not to attempt to run telecine or other 'outside' sources during these stages. However, in the next stage, *all* resources are used. (If you are not going to use telecine in the stagger through, tell the operator, so that he is not kept standing about doing nothing.)

Run through

By the end of the stagger through everybody should have a good idea of what they have to do, which parts are straightforward and which demand special care or speed. As previously mentioned, some parts may be left out for the stagger through, but everything that belongs to the final programme is used for the run through. It is an attempt to do the complete programme, without stopping, and may even be indistinguishable from the final product.

After the stagger through, give a break of say five minutes, or longer if the studio needs considerable resetting. State very clearly when you are going to start; start; watch and listen to the programme.

One good method of starting, particularly if it is the station's custom to use it for recording (q.v.) is to point a camera at a clock, set to start as 'minus 60 seconds from zero'. Monitors go to black at, say, minus ten seconds. At zero the programme starts, without further orders.

The run through has two main aims. One is to give the studio team experience of the programme as a whole rather than as disjointed parts. The other is to enable the director to judge the effect of the complete programme.

For these reasons, the team should not be stopped during the run-through, if at all possible. Of course, if the programme – perhaps because of an inadequate stagger through, simply dissolves into chaos, it *will* be necessary to stop. You should then repeat the stagger through, at least for the part that went wrong. If the original stagger through was adequate, however, it will not be necessary to stop, and you can concentrate on watching and listening to the programme. When you notice points that need to be changed, say nothing at the time, but make a note on your script. An expert director's assistant can take notes for you without interrupting the other work, but in any case the points should be written down by somebody, as one's memory is most unreliable in these circumstances.

When the programme has completed, explain the notes you have made, either through the control room talk back or by going onto the studio floor. There may be time for another run through, correcting these points, or it may now be time for line-up, stand-by, and recording.

Rehearsal for emergency direction

It may be worth while to do one rehearsal in the studio, as a check that what is being attempted is not physically impossible. Repeated rehearsals, however, do not produce a continuous improvement, as they do with systematic direction, and, indeed, often produce a deterioration as the participants tire.

The techniques used are the same as for recording – see below.

Rehearsal for observation techniques

If you are to observe behaviour, you must not rehearse with the participants you are going to use for the recording. However, it is sometimes possible to do a 'dummy run' with another group of similar people, before the people you use for the recording come in. This gives you and your staff an opportunity to find out what problems are involved before making the recording.

Allow plenty of time for the actual participants to come in and see all the equipment and (in the case of people) ask all the questions they like before you start. Provided the situation that has been organised is interesting enough, the subjects will soon lose interest in the television equipment, but can be distracted by it if you have not allowed this 'acclimatization period'. Have the lights on for all this period – don't switch them on suddenly just as you start recording.

Line up

Television equipment gives its best results if the engineers are allowed to adjust it immediately before the recording. You should therefore set aside a period when they can do this. This period is called *'line up'*. Its duration depends on the design and age of the equipment, but fifteen minutes might be reasonable for black and white equipment, thirty minutes for colour.

You should give the engineers total priority in the use of the equipment in this period, and not attempt to do any camera rehearsal. The time can usefully be spent by your team in checking that everything is ready for the recording.

At the end of line up the next stage is *stand by*. The equipment is now in the hands of the operational team, and the final checks are made. Stand by can usefully last for two minutes, with the programme starting immediately afterwards.

Possible check lists for line up and stand by follow:

Line up	*Standby*
(Engineers in charge of equipment)	(Operators in charge of equipment)
Cameras	*Cameras*
Electronic levels adjusted for best quality	All lens caps off cameras on opening shots
Camera locks on	Camera locks off
Camera cards in position in correct order	First camera card selected
All floor marks visible, headsets connected and working	Headsets connected and working. All cameramen's headsets on Floor manager's headset on Communication established with control

121

All microphones in position, connected, checked for output, faders identified

Cameras on opening marks
All talk back microphones on studio floor switched *off*

All cables routed so as not to interfere with movements of personnel and equipment. All loudspeakers in studio except fold back units switched off

Turntables
All units needed during pro-gramme switched on
Discs to be used ready in order. Faders in use on console identi-fied and closed

Tape playback
Correct tape laced to starting mark
Machine switched on – in play mode
Faders in use on console identi-fied and closed

Mixing desk
Correct level of sound being sent to VTR

Follow standby timetable

Monitors
All adjusted to same level

Vision switcher
Set to show clock as output and selected source as preview

(If required during programme) – special effects unit switched on, and first sources selected

Control room
All scripts in place and ready

Studio floor
Demonstrations in place with adequate consumables
Captions on correct stands in correct order

Talent made up, wardrobe checked

Floor manager's headset connected and functioning
Other headsets connected and functioning
Communication established between control room and floor

Recording clock running
Recording identification correctly made out,

Audio identification ready to read
Microphone for identification agreed

Telecine
Unit giving output at correct level – picture and (if necessary) sound
Machines laced with opening film
Other film ready to hand in correct order
Slides loaded in correct order

Communication established with control room

VTR
Correct tape laced for recording
Signal – video and audio – being received from studio at correct levels
Test recording carried out and of adequate quality
Insert machine(s) if needed, laced with correct tape at start marks
Machines giving correct output

Communication established with control room

Minus 1 minute	Floor manager checks all personnel present and in position Closes and locks studio doors VTR videotape machines start in record mode Audio mixer cuts tone/music to silence Transmission lights go on
– 45 sec	Floor manager calls for silence in studio
– 40 sec	Audio mixer opens mic Floor manager or assistant reads aloud information written on clock Audio mixer closes mic

123

− 10 sec	Vision mixer fades to black
0	Programme starts

Recording: systematic direction

During the recording the director's role, as previously explained, is to monitor the programme. Hopefully the complete programme will appear, exactly as required and without errors of any kind. Since the system is being run by human beings it is, however, possible that errors will occur.

If VTR editing is possible, the following options are open to the director in the event of an error.

1. Note when the error occurs and allow the programme to continue. When the programme has been completed, explain the mistake that was made, restart the recording machines and rerecord the sequence that contained the error.
   Much later the recording will be edited to eliminate the error from the programme.
2. Stop immediately the mistake is noted, reset the studio to a convenient point in the programme, and start again from there. The exact procedure for this will depend on the type of VTR editing available (see VTR editing).

Where VTR editing is not available, the only recourse is to stop the programme and start again. This can, of course, be a most time wasting business.

If the programme is being transmitted live, the situation is a very difficult one. If the error is a pedagogical one, it is possible to ask the floor manager to slip a note to the speaker asking him to correct the mistake. This is the best solution in the circumstances, but there is the considerable danger that the viewer may still remember the error rather than the corrected version. This can be used as an argument for not producing live educational television.

At the end of the programme, state quickly whether any 'retakes' are necessary, so that the studio team will not be confused as to what happens next. Make sure that the units outside the studio, such as telecine and VTR, also know what is happening and what you intend to do. If your station can do VTR editing, you may be able to record just part of the programme again to eliminate an error, in others you will have to record the whole programme again. Details of this are given on page 130 under 'VTR Editing'.

To start again you will need a *'Partial line-up'* to check the following:

Turntables
Discs ready in order from restart point
Tape playback
Correct tape laced to appropriate point
Vision switcher
Set to show clock as output
Control room
Scripts ready at restart point
Studio floor
Demonstrations in place, consumables replaced as necessary
Captions on stands in correct order from restart point
Recording clock running
Identification giving details of retake
Telecine
Machines laced with film required for beginning of retake – other
film ready to hand in correct order
Slides ready in correct order from restart point
VTR
Correct tape for retake laced for recording
Reproduce machine(s) laced with correct tape needed after restart

By using systematic direction you can watch and listen to the programme yourself, and can judge whether it is satisfactory or not. You may, too, find it a useful safeguard to have a further check from an *expert in the subject being taught* in the programme. He can sit in the control room with you, and watch and listen to the programme in the same way as you can. At the least, you will be given the confidence of his imprimatur, and he may spot a dangerous 'slip of the tongue' that you have not noticed, while there is still time to correct the error.

Once you have the complete programme recorded correctly, say so, and you will then probably have to wait for the result of a 'spot check' by VTR. This consists of a quick playback of short parts of the programme to ensure that the programme has been satisfactorily recorded in a technical sense.

Once you get confirmation of a good recording from VTR, tell your team so and thank them for the work they have done.

You can now let your studio team go home. If some VTR editing remains to be done you may prefer to arrange to do it immediately with the VTR operator or leave it until a later day.

Some producers review the entire programme as recorded on videotape before dismissing the studio. This is a good practice pedagogically, but expensive in terms of studio time and personnel. If you have used the system of direction previously described, you should have seen and heard the programme while it was being recorded and be able to give a definitive decision without the need for a playback. Nevertheless, where guests are involved, it may well be worthwhile to give them a showing of the recorded programme while the studio team are busy packing up in the studio.

It is obvious that this systematic method of direction requires considerable time in the studio. In total, 'looking at shots', the 'stagger through', and one 'run through' will absorb at least five times the total air time of the programme, and it is usual for all but the very simplest of programmes to absorb at least eight times the final air time in these stages. The operational personnel must be fairly competent, with a degree of responsibility and self discipline that permits them to work without moment-to-moment control. The programme itself must be so prepared and rehearsed that all that takes place in it is completely predictable.

Emergency direction

Each movement of the cameras, each change of shot, each change of audio is directly commanded by the director just before it is made. Listening to the director, we would hear something like this:

'Camera One, I want a medium shot of Professor Johns at the desk. Two, as soon as you are clear, go to the desk for a close-up of the model. Take One. Off you go, Two. No, Two, tighter than that. That's better. We'll cut as soon as he touches the model. Good – keep the model in the centre of frame, Two. Cut One! He's never dropped it before! Wait for him to put it back. One – tighten a little . . . Take Two – that's fine. One, be ready to cover him for a walk over to the board. Take One. Two, go and get the board. One, dolly back as he moves. That's it – faster – hold him in two-shot with the board – that's fine. Take Two. Stay there, One. Colin, have you got the closing captions ready? – put them on a stand next to Two. Grams ready with the closing music. Stand by telecine. Take One. Two, clear to the captions. One, dolly in gently to a close-up. Run telecine, up grams, mix telecine. Super Two – take it out – change caption – super Two – take it out – change caption – super Two. Ready to go to black. Fade sound and vision. That's it – thank you everybody.'

The great advantage of this system is its flexibility. The unexpected may occur during the recording – like the professor dropping his model in the example above – and the programme can keep going. This makes the system useful in cases where the action cannot be predicted exactly – when the movement of animals is being observed, for an interview, or a football game. This, and the fact that the programme can be mounted at very short notice, explains why this system is used for all news and sports programmes.

It is unlikely that the whole of the ETV programme is unpredictable, and in much ETV the need for accuracy in the programme is overwhelming. The fundamental disadvantage of the simplified system is that while the director is giving his stream of orders *he cannot monitor the programme content*. It is almost impossible to talk and listen critically at the same time, and, equally, while he is preparing a camera for its next shot, he is not viewing the shot that is on air. For all but the very simplest programmes this is a dangerous situation.

We therefore recommend that you develop your studio personnel and systems, you prepare and rehearse your participants, and that you obtain sufficient studio time so that you can use the systematic method for all except the most unpredictable sequences.

When you must use the simplified system, remember the following points:

1. Give as much forewarning as possible. Notice how, in the example given, camera Two is given the order to move to its caption as soon as camera One is selected, and not just before the caption is needed. Even better, when you can, give a warning during the previous shot – 'As soon as you finish this shot, I want you to move over to the caption stand. . . .'

2. Precede each order with the name or role of the person addressed. 'Camera Two, pan left' is unambiguous, but 'Pan left!' has been known to result in six cameras panning left together (in other studios, a chilling immobility will follow!)

3. The audio operator and the vision mixer will need to have their orders given clearly and in good time. Some vision mixing units need a little preparation before either a mix or a superimposition, and a sudden order of 'Mix Two!' may be impossible to carry out.

To avoid problems of communication, some directors using the emergency system prefer to do their own vision mixing, and equipment has even been developed so that the director can control audio and the camera movements as well. However, the use of such systems reduces even more the capability of the director to monitor the programme.

Cueing

Whichever system you are using, the presenter will need to know when to start speaking. This may be after the opening credits, or at the end of a telecine sequence in the programme.

The presenter may watch the programme monitor, and, when he

sees himself on the screen, turn to the camera and start speaking. This move, however, is usually obvious and distracting. It can be made satisfactory if the presenter has something to do – adjusting his demonstration, for example – and can continue to do this for a moment as he appears on the screen and then 'look up' at the viewer. The position of the monitor is critical for this (see page 175).

Generally the best solution to the problem is for the presenter to be given a signal by the floor manager *'cueing'* him to speak. If this signal is given to the floor manager by someone in the control room, the process 'control-floor manager-presenter-reacts and speaks' takes a little time, and so the signal needs to be given a little in advance.

In the emergency system, the director gives the order to speak before the order to cut to the relevant camera – i.e. 'cue him – and – cut.'

When a telecine or VTR sequence is running, it it useful if the director's assistant gives a 'count down' of how many minutes and seconds are left to run in the sequence. This can usefully be given every fifteen seconds and then every second for the last fifteen seconds. Those in the studio and the control room organising things for the next studio sequence will find this helpful, and it will be direct information for the vision switcher and for the floor manager.

When, in the systematic method, the duration of credits and other shots has been defined in terms of their required duration, the assistant should give 'count downs' for these, too.

An expert telecine or VTR operator can judge when to start the machine so that the first shot of the sequence appears on the screen at the right moment in the programme. For this, however, he needs an accurate script, and an opportunity to practise. Where this is impractical, the assistant can give the cue to start.

In the systematic method the shot before the presenter has to speak for the first time is usually on a time cue. The count down given by the producer's assistant gives the required information to the floor manager as to when to give his cue to the presenter. This needs practice, but is generally on about 'minus two' of the count.

A cameraman whose picture is to be *superimposed* on another needs to be able to see the superimposition before it goes on air. Some cameras have 'viewfinder mixed feed' which allows a second picture source to be connected to the cameraman's viewfinder. If you have this facility, arrange for the source which has the background to be connected to the viewfinder. With this, the cameraman can quickly adjust the picture given by his camera to fit in with the other one. If viewfinder mixed feed is not available, perhaps you can arrange for him to have a monitor showing 'Preview' and arrange with the vision mixer that this monitor show the superimposition before it is on air. If neither of these is possible, take some rehearsal time to put the superimposition on air, so that it can be seen by the studio monitor(s), and have the cameraman mark his viewfinder with wax pencil so that he knows exactly where to put his picture for the recording.

Observation techniques

Unless you are doing the camerawork yourself, and you might consider doing this – you need to explain what kind of picture you are after and to give the cameraman points of reference. A useful expression for intelligent communication with a cameraman is 'Frame up on. . . .' This means, 'Compose a picture for me with . . . as the subject of the picture.'

Good direction for observation techniques sounds like this: 'Camera 1 – pan right a bit and frame up on the child who is painting. I'd like to see what he is painting. . . . Good. Can you tighten to a close-up of the painting? Good.'

If you are using two cameras you can use one to search for examples of what you need while the other is 'on air', and you can alternate the cameras in this way. An 'off air' camera can give yes and no answers to questions by panning up and down for 'Yes', and from side to side for 'No'. You cannot use this technique with a camera that is 'on air'. Don't waste everybody's time with questions that cannot be answered, like 'What's happening?'

VTR editing

Videotape recording is one of the most rapidly developing areas of television, and the possibilities are changing almost from day to day.

It is worth talking with the engineers in charge of the VTR facilities at your station to find out what is technically possible using their equipment, particularly in the area of editing.

In radio work it is quite normal to edit an audio recording by cutting the $\frac{1}{4}$ in tape and reassembling it, either be means of a splicing block, or simply with a pair of scissors. The process is much more difficult in the case of videotape, as the *exact* place at which the tape is cut, and the angle of cut, are both important. Special units, which include microscopes, have been developed for this, but the process is falling into disuse, partly because of the high cost of the tape which is then rejected and is not available for rerecording, and partly because of the very high level of manual skill which is involved. Electronic editing is taking over.

In some stations it is possible to use one VTR machine to provide *inserts* in a programme which is being recorded by another machine, in the same way as a telecine machine is used to, provide inserts.

A VTR machine cannot give a picture immediately it is requested. A certain time must elapse between the pressing of the 'play' button and the appearance of a stable, usable picture on the screen. Depending on the design of the machine, this 'run up' time may be as short as a second or as long as a minute. The time is, however, constant for any particular machine. Find out what the run up time is for the machines that you will be using, and arrange for you or your assistant to give the order to VTR with the correct anticipation so that the picture can be switched into your programme at the instant required.

It is also worth finding out whether the signal from VTR permits mixes or split screen effects from the studio, or whether only cutting is technically possible.

Sometimes editing is possible using just one machine. Suppose that while a programme is being recorded, an error occurs in shot 23. The producer stops the recording, and asks the studio to get ready to record again, starting at (say) shot 22. The VTR machine is run back to an earlier point – say shot 19 – and set running in playback. The playback continues to the end of shot 21 and then is switched – without stopping – to record. The studio programme is now running again, and continues from shot 22.

You can see that the success of this technique depends on exact synchronism between the VTR and the studio. Most VTR machines have very accurate counters, and after some preparation the operator will be able to give an exact countdown to the point at which recording starts. The director or his assistant uses this countdown to give a signal to the studio to restart just before the switch to record is made. With practice, this process can provide a technique whereby a technically perfect programme can be built up step by step. In normal use, however, it is more time consuming than you might expect, mainly because of the time needed to set up VTR and to organise the countdown accurately.

The *jig-saw assembly* technique is to take segments from one or more tapes and assemble them, in the required order, onto a final tape. Any number of starts and stops can thus be made in the recording, which can even be made 'shot by shot'. Time in the studio is more efficiently used than in the previous technique, but the assembly afterwards can be very time consuming. The process of assembly is helped if you have an assistant who can take notes of suitable and unsuitable sequences recorded as you go along.

For a recording made by observation techniques you must sit down with the subject specialist and decide between you which part(s) of the recording show the behaviour you need to show.

8 Transmission techniques

The way in which the programme is transmitted and/or shown to an audience depends very much on the kind of system you are working with.

In many countries, *commercial television channels* give airtime for the transmission of instructional television. If your programme is to be transmitted in this way, you should bear in mind that exact timing is very important to a commercial station. If exactly fifteen minutes have been donated to instructional TV, the programme may well be cut off, completed or not, at 15 min 5 sec. If the programme stops short at 14 min 35 sec, the commercial station may be equally annoyed. Find out if the commercial station is sensitive in this way. If it is, then you will have to make your programmes to exactly the length they require. In the preparation of the programme keep an eye on the total duration, particularly during dry rehearsals, modifying the programme as necessary. To bring the programme duration to exactly the time required, you can adjust the duration of the final credits.

Instructional TV stations are usually much less sensitive about the duration of the programme. However, where the programme is used at organised centres of reception and its use is integrated with the activities of a classroom teacher or 'monitor', synchronisation with his activities *is* important. The classroom teacher needs to know exactly how much time he has left to complete his introduction to the programme, and it is useful to him to have some reassurance that everything is in order, and that the next programme is indeed the one he is expecting. We suggest the use of a broadcast clock for at least

131

five minutes before the programme starts – indeed up to fifteen minutes can profitably be used if available.

Any large clear clock showing the present time may be put on the screen, though it is perhaps more useful to use a backward-running clock that indicates the time remaining before the programme starts. A stand can be built to house the clock, and other useful information can be given on a board to one side of the clock and/or the clock can be incorporated in a receiver line up pattern.

Some *closed circuit systems* run in just the same way as the broadcast station, and some may even run like a commercial station, in which case the corresponding techniques are used. With the advent of relatively cheap videocassette machines, however, there is a tendency to distribute these machines widely and lend tapes as one would lend books or films at other libraries. Programmes must then be of such a length that they will fit conveniently onto the cassettes available, and accurate labelling is of great importance, as the distribution of the tapes or cassettes may be controlled by those who have no way of checking whether the correct programme is being supplied, other than by its label.

It is most important that you attend the *showing of your programme* in one of the viewing centres. Take careful note of how the audience reacts. Are there parts of the programme in which the viewers' attention wanders? Look out for the level of noise made by the viewers – shuffling of feet, coughs, and talking are all symptoms that the programme is failing to hold attention. Some programmes can hold a large audience completely silent. However, with some cultures and some kinds of programme, the audience may respond to the presenter, perhaps answering questions. Does this happen smoothly? Are the answers clear or confused? Does the presenter allow sufficient time for the answers?

If you can get permission from the person in charge of the class, talk with the pupils after the lesson and find out, as far as you can, whether or not the objectives were achieved. The better the construction of the objectives, the easier it is to check this.

A full evaluation includes not only testing after a programme – the post test – but pre-testing as well. It involves choosing sample groups from the total audience and testing to show that these groups are representative of the whole. If you have a competent evaluation team doing all this, they should be able to give you full information on the achievement of the objectives. If your programme was structured accordingly, you should be able to identify the parts of your programme which were successful and those which were not.

This is your best guide as to how to remake the programme and how to make further programmes of the same type.

132

Evaluation

To *react constructively* to programme evaluation is one of the most difficult tasks for a programme producer. During the production of the programme he becomes accustomed to insisting on his concept of the way in which the programme should be made. So that the programme shall be completed at all, he has had to make it clear that although there are several ways in which it could be made, it must be done his way – any other approach is likely to produce incoherence at best and total confusion at worst. Suddenly he has to turn round, listen to 'criticism' of the way he has done the programme, and consider alternative plans of action.

This psychological turnround is, however, absolutely necessary. So little is at present known about the mechanisms of learning and communication that the best approach is one of responsible trial and error. The production team makes the best programme it can within the production limitations and given the resources and information at its disposal. To identify the parts of the programme that were successful and those which were not is a vital task and the only way to plan responsibly for the future.

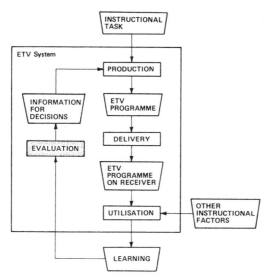

The instructional television system – evaluation.

The reason for having a system is to produce a *change*.

Thus, you can measure the efficacy of a system best by measuring the change it produces.

Behavioural objectives are useful for this, because they define an

133

observable behaviour which the viewer will be able to show after the learning experience.

What do you want the viewer to be able to do? Could he do it before viewing the programme? Can he do it after viewing the programme?

Evaluators often answer these questions by means of written tests, and this can be a convenient method if large numbers of viewers are involved. Do not forget, however, that the behaviour you are trying to produce may not involve written skills. In the example of the television receiver programme, it is less important whether a viewer can answer a written examination about the receiver (he could be illiterate) as whether, given a receiver, he can produce a picture from it.

What kind of information will help you to improve your programme?

If you were told that a test conducted on your programme showed a mean mark of 70%, what would that mean to you? What would you do about the programme? Would you leave it as it was? Is 70% a good mark?

Imagine that this programme had three objectives and that each objective had been evaluated separately, as follows:

Objective 1 – 100% of students achieved
Objective 2 – 100% of students achieved
Objective 3 – 10% of students achieved
Mean mark 70%

It is now obvious what you have to do – improve the part of the programme that dealt with Objective 3. Beward of reacting to mean marks. Insist on evaluation of each of your objectives so that you can see precisely which parts of the programme need improving.

What about objectives 1 and 2? Would you be happy about these? You should not be. You do not know whether the audience already had the ability to achieve these objectives before watching your programme. Perhaps a test given before the programme was viewed would have given these results:

	Pre-test	(Post-test)
Obj. 1	100	(100)
Obj. 2	0	(100)
Obj. 3	10	(10)

In fact, there was no need for the part of the programme that dealt with objective 1. You could leave it out and devote more resources to the problem of Objective 3 which is even more serious than it appeared at first.

Unless you are sure that there is no possibility that your audience already knows what you are teaching you should have the results of a pre-test to compare with the post-test.

Are you satisfied with the results?

Do not expect 100% results. There will almost certainly be random errors by some learners.

How much should you allow for errors? This depends on the student and upon the objective. Is the objective something that is so important that it *must* be achieved? Is the audience homogeneous?

Both you and the evaluator must agree as to the *validity* of the evaluation.

Ask to see any test *before* it is applied. Answer the questions on the test yourself. Can you understand the questions? Is this what you expected a learner would be able to do? Will the responses of the learner to these questions help you to improve the programme?

To what extent are the people who will be tested representative of the whole audience? Is the test situation representative of the situations for which the programme is designed?

Are other media involved with television in achieving the instructional objectives? How can the effects of the television programme be separated from the effects of the other elements? You might need to use a control group who do not use television, and compare the results.

Do not rely solely on the results of formal testing. Sit with learners as they watch the programme. Note when attention is lost or where reactions are not what you expected or wanted. Talk informally with the learners. Ask about each of the programme elements.

Some systems have an 'evaluation' process after the programme has been made and before it is transmitted. Educational specialists study the programme to evaluate its style. They ask such questions as 'Was the presenter sincere?' 'Did he speak too slowly or too quickly?' 'Were the graphics clear?'

This is an extremely irritating practice. Any criticism or evaluation of this kind, if it has to take place, should be done before recording so that you can take it into account.

Anybody who knows better than the production team should be in it!

The only kind of evaluation which is valid after a programme has been recorded and before it is transmitted is when a programme is pre-tested with a sample of the real audience.

9 Appendix I

Design of shots for instructional TV

The mnemonic FASTDOTS can be used to design the necessary shots for instruction. FASTDOTS stand for:

F Fine detail   The low definition of the television system prevents it from showing fine detail, so necessary detail must be shown as large as possible.

A Area lost   However, not all the picture area scanned by the television system is seen by the viewer, so we have to work inside a "safe area".

S Size information   The television image by itself gives no information as to the absolute size of the object being shown, so it is frequently necessary to make comparisons with known objects.

T Third dimension   Neither does the image give information as to the depth of what is being shown, though lighting and perspective can create the necessary illusion.

D Distraction   Extraneous detail can distract the viewer's attention, particularly if it is moving.

O	Opposition	Contradictions, real or apparent, inside the picture or between picture and sound, can be confusing and distracting.
T	Tints	Colour information can be distorted in the various stages of a colour television system or may be lost altogether in a system that is partly or wholly monochrome. Picture contrast must be adequate between parts of the picture that need to be distinguished.
S	Setting	The viewer does not necessarily know the visual context of what is being shown, and you may have to organize additional pictures to show him this.

FASTDOTS can be used as a rapid check on any picture to be shown on television.

Often the requirements cannot be met by a *single* picture.

Suppose you need to show a kind of butterfly unknown to the viewer. Analyse the following pictures in terms of FASTDOTS. Try this for yourself before reading on.

Picture A   Picture B
Compare the two for teaching effectiveness.

Picture A

Fine detail	Hardly any – on a television screen no details of the butterfly will be seen.
Area lost	OK. All essential information is within the "safe area".
Size	OK. The comparison with the demonstrator establishes the size of the butterfly.
Third dimension	Information will be given if the demonstrator moves the butterfly.
Distraction	OK. Only essential information is shown.

Opposition	None.	
Tints	A problem – if the colour is essential, and a monochrome system is being used, it will have be explained in some way.	
Setting	No problem, unless you need to show that the demonstrator is in some particular place.	

Picture B

Fine detail	Much better than A – the viewer should be able to see the layout of the wings, though smaller detail such as the antennae is still too small.
Area lost	No problem.
Size	No information – from this one shot it would be assumed that the insect was the size of an elephant or as small as the head of a pin.
Third dimension	No information unless it is moved.
Distraction	None.
Opposition	None.
Tints	As before.
Setting	No information.

Each shot has its advantages and disadvantages. By using *both* shots, you could combine the advantages of each.

	Picture A	Picture B	Combination A+B
F	No	OK	OK
A	OK	OK	OK
S	OK	No	OK
T	No	No	OK*
D	OK	OK	OK
O	OK	OK	OK
T	?	?	?
S	?	No	?

*If Pictures A and B are taken from different angles, the different views of the insect in the two shots do give some information on the third dimension.

138

It is possible to give the illusion to *each* viewer that the presenter is speaking to him and to him alone. This is made possible by the fact that you are showing a three dimensional object – the presenter's face – on a two dimensional screen. The effect is produced by the presenter looking at the camera lens in use while he is speaking. It is an important technique, and one that should be practised.

The size of the image of the face also affects the contact between presenter and viewer.

Shots for showing one person

This shot – what we shall call a medium shot – has rather less impact on the viewer than

this 'close-up'.

This extreme close-up probably has too much impact for most faces, though it can be used for grotesque or frightening effect in a drama.

The relative heights of the camera and presenter can also have some psychological effect, i.e.:

Camera above presenter – sense of inferiority or insecurity

Camera below presenter – sense of superiority and dominance.

In looking at *objects* in the studio, we first need to establish the size of the object. In the studio, the presenter himself forms a good standard of comparison for medium sized objects, and if he can handle the objects he can show various aspects of it by moving it about. We start, then, with a two-shot of the presenter and the object.

Immediately we meet differences between classroom and studio technique. A classroom teacher is used to holding an object high in the air – so that the view of any pupil is not blocked by the pupil in front of him – and moving it about. This technique has no advantage in the case of television, and gives problems to the cameraman who is trying to keep the object in shot.

In a classroom it is best to hold an object up, *in television, it is better to down it* down, *and not to move it from place to place.*

Usually, you will need a support for the object, be it a table, a stand, or some sort of suspension.

Again, if a teacher is to show something on a table, it is a normal technique to stand behind the table and demonstrate the object from there. This avoids the view of a pupil from being blocked by the teacher's body.

On television, however, the result would be a shot like this:

Both the presenter's face and the object are small on the screen, and not much of the screen is being purposefully used. Since this is a low definition medium we wish to show both of these as large as possible.

It is thus better to raise the object (or lower the presenter) so that the two are at the same level, and put them side by side. This allows a larger image of each:

This is an adequate two-shot, clearly showing the relationship between presenter and object, and making good use of the screen area (inside the safe area).

After this introduction to the object, we need to concentrate on it, in order to see it in detail. Once the size has been established, the presenter becomes irrelevant, and we need a picture of the object alone:

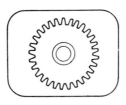

what we will call a close-up of the object.

How do we obtain the two shots that we need – the establishing two-shot and the close-up. How do we change from one to the other?

Single camera techniques

1. *Track in*

It is possible to start with the camera at a distance from the presenter, and then move it closer so that the screen is filled with the image of the object.

This is quite practicable, but the following problems arise:

a. With a zoom lens, it is difficult to hold focus during the movement.
   With a turret camera, the use of a narrow angle lens gives an unsteady movement on the screen, but a wide angle lens may need to be inconveniently close to the object at the end of the track.

b. The move takes time, and we may be making the viewer wait for an adequate view of the object.

c. At some point in the move, only part of the presenter's body will be seen. This may not distract during the track in, when the viewer knows what he is looking at, but may distract (as with temporarily unidentified objects) if you wish to do a track out at the end of the demonstration.

2. *Zoom in*

Similarly, we can use a camera with a zoom lens, and zoom in from the two-shot to the close-up.

Compared with the track in, this eliminates problem 'a' alone, since the zoom in can certainly be made sufficiently smooth, and at the end of the zoom, the lens is effectively a narrow angle one, not needing to be inconveniently near to the object.

However, the other two problems, 'b' and 'c' still exist.

3. *Move the object*

An extreme solution favoured by some producers is for the presenter to pick up the object and thrust it towards the lens. If the lens is a wide angle one, or a zoom at a wide angle setting the cameraman may be able to hold focus, and thus give a close-up of the object.

However, it is a difficult and risky process, as the focus is very critical at short distances and the presenter may find it very difficult to hold the object sufficiently still. There is also likely to be a lighting problem.

Multi-camera techniques

We may use one camera for the two-shot, and another for the close-up. This is an important television technique, and one that we shall discuss in detail.

Firstly, is it necessary for each camera to look at the *same* object? In most work this may well be so, but if there are two identical objects available, we may use one of them for the two-shot, and the other for the close-up.

This technique is valuable when the object presents special lighting problems, or when it is particularly small. The difficulties are obviously those of matching the two shots — making the background to the object identical in each case, making sure that a finger (say) touching the object in one shot does not suddenly disappear in the

142

next, and so on. In the succeeding discussion we shall assume that the *same* object is used for both shots.

If we use two cameras on the same object, one to produce the two-shot and the other the close-up, the positioning of the two cameras becomes critical.

Positioning of the cameras

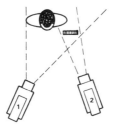

This is a plan view of one possible arrangement of the two cameras, the presenter and the object.

In this case, camera 1, with a wide angle lens, is taking the two-shot, and camera 2, with a narrow angle lens, the close-up.

The two pictures look like this:

With these two pictures we can certainly meet our original aims – to establish the size of the object and then to show it in sufficient detail but neither shot is yet perfect.

A difficulty with the two-shot arises when the presenter has to indicate the object. In the arrangement shown, he must turn considerably away from the viewer, in order to do this. This is uncomfortable, and prejudices the apparent contact between presenter and viewer.

A second problem arises in the close-up. Behind the object we can see the body of the presenter. This is sufficiently distracting in the 'still' diagram as it is difficult to identify immediately, but on the screen will be even worse, as it will be moving, if only slightly, and a moving object generally distracts attention from a stationary one.

The alternative is to interchange the roles of the two cameras, like this:

The angle through which the presenter now has to turn to look at the object from the camera is much reduced, and camera 1 has a clear view of the object, with no distractions in the background.

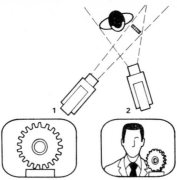

Notice how the axes of the two cameras intersect in front of the presenter. The arrangement is called 'cross-shooting' and is one that we shall meet again.

A similar problem occurs if we wish the presenter to show detail on a large flat surface, such as a chart or a map.

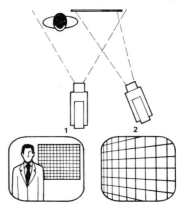

In this arrangement, we have similar difficulties. The presenter has to turn through nearly ninety degrees to point at the display, and the close-up produced by camera 2 is distorted, as the camera is not square-on to the display.

The presenter can now make his turn much more easily; we are no longer requiring him to point out something that is behind him. Camera 1, square on to the display, produces an undistorted image.

True, the image of the display in the two-shot is 'distorted', but the eye and brain accept this without difficulty as part of the general scene.

There is one exception to the cross-shooting rule.

In each of the cases so far, the aim has been to display the object efficiently and without distraction. The view seen by the presenter himself is not the same as that seen by the camera, but this is not important.

We reverse the cameras' roles, and cross-shoot:

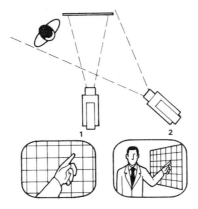

When some skill is being demonstrated which involves a 'left and right' orientation – for example, tying a knot – you need a 'subjective camera' technique. This consists of shots which give the same view of what is happening as the 'operator' has. The viewer's 'right' and the operator's 'right' are the same.

This can be difficult to organise.

If the programme is teaching how to type, the viewer needs to see the movement of the fingers over the keyboard, but most of the camera's possible lines of sight are blocked by the demonstration

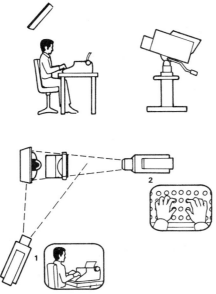

Mirror used to give 'user's view' of keyboard (see text).

typist. If you have very small cameras, or a big one on a crane with a long focus lens, you can arrange for a camera to peer over the demonstrator's shoulder.

If you cannot avoid the camera appearing in the establishing shot, and it is large enough to be distracting, you can try the technique mentioned earlier and use two typewriters and have one person as presenter and another as demonstrator. Another method is to suspend a mirror above the keyboard and have the close-up camera look into this. The image in the mirror is reversed either laterally or vertically, but this can be corrected in the electronics of the camera to give a image which is the right way round.

Two people

For a discussion between two people, we can again apply the FASTDOTS rule to decide what shots we need.

F ine detail	For each person we need to see them sufficiently large to be able to discern the detail that distinguishes them from others – see section on single person.
A rea lost	The above is limited by safe area considerations.
S ize	Though we know roughly how large a human being is likely to be, some comparison may be useful.
T ints	No major problem.
D istraction	Many possibilities – see later.
O opposition	See later.
T hird dimension	No major problem.
S etting	We want to know the relationship of the people to each other.

Once again, these requirements can be met by a sequence of shots: a two-shot, or individual close-ups.

A feeling of participation in their discussion would be obtained by eye contact with each person as he speaks. Since he is probably looking at the person to whom he is speaking, this cannot be obtained exactly without each camera taking the place of each speaker in turn – impractical in television, though practical and often used in studio

146

filming. A near compromise in television is to place the cameras like this:

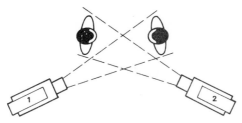

Over-shoulder cross-shooting (two-shot).

Intercutting between cameras (pairs of shots).

The shots in any one of these pairs can be intercut when the participants speak.

Usually we cut to the person who is talking – though a reaction shot – that is, one of the person who is listening – can be effective if used sparingly. If you are going to use reaction shots, though, the interviewer must be warned so that you do not catch him looking away from the guest when he is on air.

The following arrangement is physically possible, but gives a misleading effect:

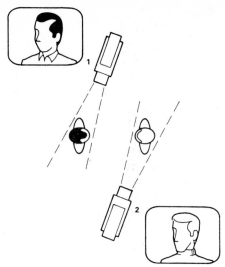

Effect of placing cameras on opposite sides of 'line of action'.

Notice that in the two pictures of the participants, they appear to be looking in the same direction. Thus we have lost the effect that they are looking at each other. This occurs when the cameras are on opposite sides of the imaginary line joining the participants – a line sometimes called the 'line of action'.

Actually, this error occurs very rarely in a discussion set, but it is something to be remembered in drama.

Notice, too, that in the arrangement shown on page 147 the cameras are again cross-shooting. If the cameras do not cross shoot, we get this arrangement:

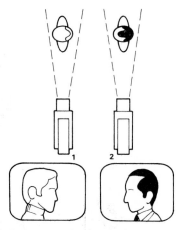

Effect of placing cameras to provide two profile shots.

With the cameras side by side and not cross-shooting, they must be side-on to the participants. Since they look at each other while talking, this means that they are never close to looking at the viewer. The result is a loss of the sense of participation which is a feature of the result of proper cross-shooting.

Look again at the arrangement on page 147 and compare the result with what we have just seen.

Picture composition

Notice, too, how the pictures are composed. A less experienced cameraman might arrange the pictures so that the head is centred in the frame.

In practice, this gives a rather disturbing effect, almost as if the two participants were sitting back to back — try it in the studio and see. It seems better to arrange the composition so that the *nose* of each person is on the centre line.

You may have a little difficulty in getting the right *camera height*. With many camera mounts, the result of using the camera at its lowest position with the participants seated in ordinary chairs is to show an area of floor and/or the bottom edge of the scenery. This can form a distracting background, quite apart from the unwanted psychological effect of looking *down* on the participants. Raising the camera only makes matters worse. The usual solution is to put the two chairs on a large platform. This has the effect of raising the participants, permits the cameras to look horizontally rather than downwards, and solves the problem of the background.

If the *chairs* are placed at an angle to each other, this produces a more relaxed looking situation than when the chairs are 'head on', which gives a rather interrogatory effect. If you give the participants

149

swivelling chairs, they will probably instinctively rotate them to natural-looking positions! If possible, get comfortable chairs, but they should be straightbacked so that the participants do not lean backwards, causing focus problems and shots with exaggerated tummies.

It is quite difficult to get a *microphone* boom into a good position for the discussion set. It must be close enough so as to be able to pick up the low level, conversational voices, yet, because the boom microphone is directional, it must be able to swivel to pick up each voice in turn. If each of the participants is accustomed to their use, Lavalier microphones can be used, and another solution is to use stand microphones. These can be installed easily, since it is obvious precisely where each participant will be. Elegant stand microphones can appear in shot for this kind of situation.

These, then are the ways to make sequences for the most common situations – the presenter by himself, presenter/demonstrator with object, and interaction between two people.

A programme generally contains a number of sequences, so we need methods of making the *transition from one sequence to another*.

There are four major methods:

1. Transfer to, and from, third source
2. Separate clearing of cameras
3. Walk in shot
4. Editing.

Transfer to third source

If one scene occupies two cameras, and another comes from a third source, the transition is simple. For example:

C2	CU model
C1	MS Presenter
MIX TC	Sequence B: Cranes.

The final shot of one scene is dissolved into the first shot of the next scene, which is on film, in telecine. While the film is running, the two cameras can move to their positions for the scene after that.

A dissolve is frequently used for this kind of change, emphasising the change of time and/or place involved. A straight cut can be used, if this will not cause confusion. A fade to black and a fade to the film is a way of emphasising the change still further. A wipe is technically possible, but may prove very distracting. A popular technique in commercial television is to put the film onto the presenter's background by means of chroma key, and then zoom into the background. This usually gives the visual effect of the presenter sliding *forward*, a potent distraction.

150

Separate clearing of cameras

In this technique the two cameras, when not required on air, move off in turn to the next scene.

C2	CU model
C1	MS Presenter
C2	CU Crane
C1	MS Presenter and crane

(A straight cut is employed in this example, but a dissolve could be used to emphasise the change.)

This is one possible arrangement:

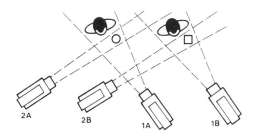

The following is possible, and permits a very quick change for the cameras, though it involves a longer, and possibly awkward, move for the presenter:

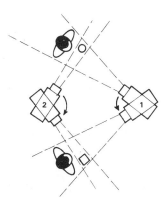

The following, however, is not possible, other than in a discontinuous recording (stopping the recorder and/or editing after the second shot):

Camera 1 cannot get from 1A to 1B without appearing in camera 2's shot (unless the cables are so arranged as to enable it to go round the back of camera 2!)

151

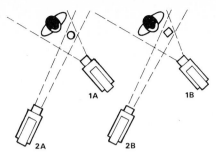

Separate clearing of the cameras is much used when credits are involved, e.g.:

C2	CU Model
C1	MS Presenter
C2	Credit y
C1	Credit x

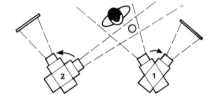

and this can be used for superimpositions —

C2	CU Model
C1	2-S Presenter and model
C2	CU Model
C1 and C2	C1 Credit 'MODEL' C2 CU Model
C2	CU Model
C1	MS Presenter

Walk in shot

In this technique, the presenter walks from one scene to the next, while still in shot.

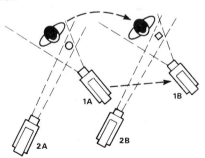

152

C2   CU Model

C1 2-S Presenter and model Dolly back as presenter walks forward to 2S Presenter and Crane

C2   . CU Crane

Notice how the presenter walks roughly towards the camera; a walk away from the camera feels, and looks, awkward.

This change is best carried out with cameras that can move smoothly – i.e. cameras mounted on pedestals or cranes. An approximation is, however, possible with static cameras and zoom lenses:

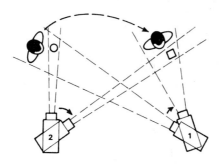

With mobile cameras, the change can be repeated as many times as necessary, or at least until you run out of studio space:

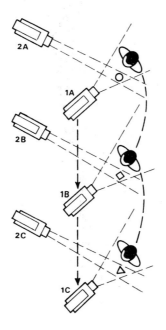

Editing

When VTR or film editing is available, the programme can be recorded scene by scene, and you only have to be careful that the presenter does not appear in consecutive shots:

CU   Model

MS   Presenter and model

Stop recording and restart at new positions

CU   Crane   (not 2–S or presenter will "jump"
                        from one place to another)

MS   Presenter and crane

Advanced techniques

The techniques just described – how to show a person and an object, how to show the interaction of two people, and how to transfer from one scene to another – cover most instructional television. Once you have mastered these, you can go on to the more advanced techniques of drama, as described in various books on the subject.

These techniques can be used however you are to make a sequence, whether by OB unit or studio, by filming or VTR recording, with, and without editing.

10   Appendix II

Lighting

What follows is an account of how some simple situations often found in ETV productions can be lit.

Some stations have no trained lighting engineers, and this account can be used as a guide for setting up the lights.
Even if you have trained staff to organise and set up the lighting you should still read this section. As you will see, the lighting required is very dependent on the way the studio floor is organised. A producer with some basic knowledge of lighting techniques can make life very much easier for the lighting engineer – thus producing better pictures and a better working atmosphere!

Lamps

A well equipped studio has lamps of many different types. If a lamp is going to be used as part of the lighting of a television production, two facts about it are important. One is its power, and the other is whether it gives a 'hard' or a 'soft' light.

Power

This is simply the electrical power used by the lamp. Most studios have lamps of 750 watts and of 1,000 watts (written as 1 kw), and large studios have more powerful lamps of 5 kw or 10 kw. Not all of this power is converted into light; most lamps convert a lot of the power into heat, and dispersing this heat is a major problem in many television studios.

Hard and soft light

Many people find this a confusing concept, but it is worth careful study to understand the difference, as it is crucial to the way a set is lit. It is best understood by means of a demonstration. When you are in the studio, ask an engineer to light a spot lamp and point it at a plain surface – say the studio wall or a 'cyclorama'. Hold up your hand so that its shadow falls on this surface. The shadow is bold, well defined, and most noticeable. This is called a 'hard' shadow. Light that produces a hard shadow is called hard light. Lamps that produce a hard light are small in size, or have optical systems to give the same effect.

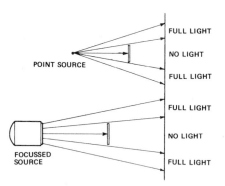

Hard shadows in television lighting.

In a studio, the sources of hard light are the spotlights.

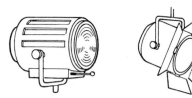

The spotlight – referred to by the power of its bulb – be it 750 watt, 1 kw, 5 kw, or 10 kw – has a focusing control, a swivelling and locking support, and often has movable flaps – 'barn doors' – to control the spread of light. It provides no means of controlling the *intensity* of the light – apart from an on-off switch. The intensity is controlled by dimmers in a separate control panel.

Now switch off the spotlight and switch on a large lamp – say a fluorescent strip lamp. You may now find it difficult to produce a noticeable shadow at all. If a shadow is produced (to do this the light

156

will have to be quite close to the surface) it will be weak and diffuse, what we call a 'soft' shadow. The light is thus called 'soft' light.

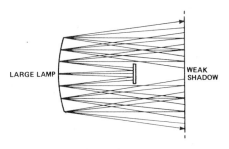

The only lamps that can give soft light are those that are physically large. The size of a lamp should not be confused with its power. A powerful spot lamp (and in particular an arc lamp) can be quite small, yet it gives a great deal of light – hard light. A large fluorescent lamp may give relatively little light. Because of its size, however, that light will be soft.

It is quite difficult to fit large lamps into the confined space of a television studio. Fluorescent lamps give problems in colour studios because their light is a markedly different colour from that of conventional incandescent lamps. The nearest approach to a source of soft light that is usually found in a television studio is the 'ten light' (or tenlite).

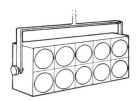

No focusing arrangement is provided on such units, though they occasionally have barn doors to limit the spread of light.

A compromise is a unit called a 'scoop'. This has a single bulb and a circular matt reflector. Scoops are rather smaller than a ten light and thus give a harder light. To produce a soft light it is necessary to use them in pairs or triplets.

Diffusors – say sheets of translucent fibreglass – can be fitted in front of scoops to soften the light further.

Combinations: hard and soft light

In ordinary daylight, objects are illuminated by a combination of hard and soft light. The hard light comes directly from the sun, which is seen from the Earth as a 'small' object. This hard light produces clearly defined shadows. In a two-dimensional representation of an object lit by daylight, these shadows give us information on the three dimensional nature of the object. We say that the hard light has a modelling effect on the object.

However, the shadows produced by the light from the sun are not intensely black, because the light from the rest of the sky – a source of soft light – fills them in to some extent without producing shadows of its own.

In a studio, we use a similar combination of hard and soft light.

The first example we shall consider is that of a human face looking straight at the camera.

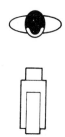

The lamp used to produce the modelling effect is called the 'modelling light', or, more often, the 'key light'. As we are trying to produce shadows, it is logical to use a source of hard light, such as a spotlight for this. Different positions of this key light, relative to the line joining camera and subject, give different effects. If the light is too near this axis, the shadows are small and little modelling is achieved. If the angles are great, large areas of shadow are formed, giving a very dramatic effect. While the latter may be useful for some kinds of drama, a normal 'talking head' shot requires that eye contact must not be lost by shadows in the eye areas, and this limits the angle used. For convenience, the lamp can be placed at some 30 degrees horizontally from the line joining the camera to the face, and at some 30 degrees to the horizontal.

Actually determining these angles in the studio may be a little troublesome; a horizontal angle of 30 degrees may be drawn on the

158

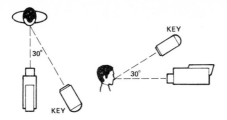

floor plan with a protractor or setsquare, but the vertical angle is a little more. An easy rule of thumb is that the distance of the keylight
from the subject should be twice the amount that the light is higher
than the subject. For example if the lamp is two metres above the
presenter's head, the distance from presenter to lamp should be four
metres. This rule applies exactly to the straightline distance from head
to lamp, but if the horizontal distance is used the angle becomes about
27 degrees, which is near enough.

The same rule can be used for the horizontal angle:

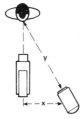

x is half y, i.e. if the distance y is 6 metres, x should be 3 metres.

We now have adequate modelling for the face. For a few masculine
faces this is sufficient, and it may also be sufficient if we want a contrasty effect, for example, for a night scene. However, it is usually a
more natural effect if the contrast of the scene is reduced by partly filling the shadows. If we use another hard light to do this, the second
light will produce a second set of shadows. This is an unusual effect in
real life, and the result is unnatural. The 'fill light' must, then, be soft
light.

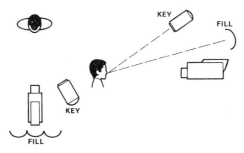

Soft light, as we saw, is produced by large light sources, say by a 'ten light'. The best position, in order to produce no secondary shadows, is exactly on the line of the camera to subject, but this is obviously inconvenient for the cameraman. One compromise is to place it on the horizontal line of camera to face, but slightly above head height.

Another arrangement is to put the fill light on the other side of the camera-subject axis to the key light.

This arrangement is rather more flexible than the one before, allowing a certain amount of movement of either the subject or the camera.

The difference in brightness between the key light and the fill light needs consideration. If the brightness of the fill is inadequate, the result is too contrasty, whereas too bright a fill can destroy the modelling effect of the key light, or even, if it is very bright and is to one side of the face, produce a sort of 'reverse modelling', the side nearer the fill being brighter than that nearer the key. Thus the brightness of the key light critically controls the contrast of the face. If your studio is equipped with light dimmers, it is worth having the fill connected through a dimmer. You can then select the exact setting you want by watching the effect on a monitor as the dimmer is adjusted. In a studio without dimmers life is a little more complicated. If the fill has several internal light sources, as is the case with the ten light, some of these can be switched off or otherwise disconnected to reduce the amount of light produced. If it is a pair of scoops, switching off one of them will probably result in a light that is too hard. However, extra layers of diffuser may be fitted, or the distance from face to light can be reduced – doubling the distance reduces the brightness on the face to about a quarter.

In these diagrams we have shown the lamp for the key light at camera right, and the lamp for the fill light on the left. This relation is not important; in this simple situation it gives equally good results to put the key on the left and the fill on the right.

However, the choice of position for the key light will have repercussions later on. For example, suppose the microphone boom is placed on the same side of the camera as the key light.

160

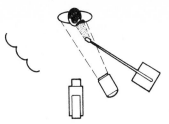

The key light casts a strong shadow of the microphone onto the actor's face. Either the microphone or the key light must be moved.

In this case, the microphone is on the side of the fill light, which, being soft, does not cast noticeable shadows.

A useful technique is now to add a hard light from behind the subject, shining onto the back of his head and his shoulders. This
produces an attractive 'rim' of light around the head and shoulders,
effectively separating the subject from the background. Some lighting
engineers use a single spotlamp for this –

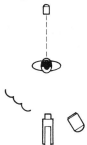

Others use two, at some 20° to the line joining camera and actor.

161

In each case the angle of elevation of the 'back light' is important. If the light is too low, there is a danger that it will shine directly into the lens of the camera, possibly causing damage, and certainly degrading the image. If it is too high, it may cause distracting bright patches on the face. Usually it can be two to three times as far from the head as its height above it.

It may be that the background is adequately lit by 'spill' light from the lamps we have already arranged. However, better control is obtained by using separate lamps to light the background. Depending on the effect required, such lamps may be small spotlights, scoops or ten lights, or may even be 'effects' spots, which cast a pattern of light on the background.

To light this scene, a face in front of a background, we have thus used lights in four different ways – as key light, filler, back light, and background light.

As was the case with the fill light, the intensities of the back light and the background light can be varied to produce different effects. Too little back light, and the subject (particularly the top of the head) will tend to merge into the background. Too much, and the effect is rather ethereal – in extreme cases, the video engineer may have difficulty in keeping the scene within the required limits without darkening the face too much. Varying the background light level also changes the 'atmosphere' of the scene. All these changes should be practised in the studio, if possible.

The following paragraphs deal with rather more complicated lighting arrangements. Preferably the reading of these sections should be accompanied by some practical work in the studio.

Presenter and board

This may be a lecturer with a large map, an art expert with a painting, or even a teacher with a blackboard. It is an arrangement that frequently causes difficulties in the ETV studio, as at first sight there seems to be no way of avoiding shadows on the flat surface.

In the diagram, the presenter is in front of the blackboard. The key light is at thirty degrees to the line joining presenter and camera, and whether it be to left or right, the presenter will cast a shadow on the

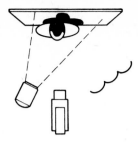

board. This is particularly distracting when the presenter points to something on the board.

However, that is merely yet another reason for *not* having the presenter stand directly in front of the board. As we saw on page 144, it is far better to have him to one side.

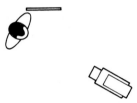

Now the key light can come in along the line of the board.

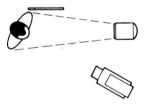

And the filler can be on the other side.

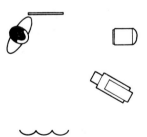

Notice how the board is now illuminated only by soft light. There cannot now be any distracting shadows on it, provided the filler is truly soft light. If, as in the case of the light produced by a pair of scoops, the light is not entirely soft, a shadow will be produced.

163

Notice, however, that if the fill light is on the same line as the camera, the shadow will fall *behind* the hand (say) producing it, and will not be seen. In critical situations, get the fill light as near to the camera as possible.

The second camera can now be at right angles to the board.

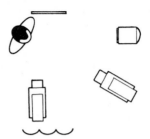

We can now add a back light for the presenter, something that was impossible with the original arrangement.

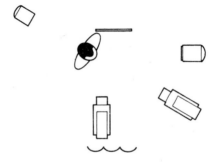

And the background behind him is lit separately.

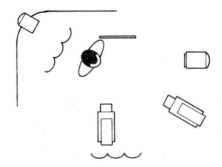

Presenter with object

A very similar arrangement can be used for a presenter showing an object.

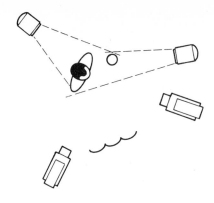

For this diagram, the object has taken the place of the board. By adjusting the positions of the key light and the second camera slightly, the presenter's key light can be made to serve also as a backlight for the object – thus helping to distinguish it from its background. Notice that the back light for the presenter acts as a key light for the object. However, this needs some care; if the object is too low in relation to the presenter it will fall in the shadow cast by his back light. With the object and the presenter at about the same height, this problem is avoided.

As before, the background is lit separately.

Interview

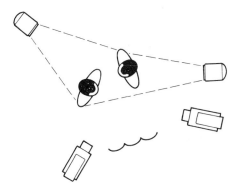

This arrangement is almost identical to that for 'presenter with object'. Each of the spotlamps is dual function, acting as backlight for one of the participants and as keylight for the other. The background is lit separately.

Drama

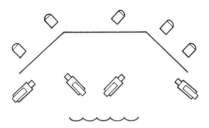

Lighting for drama can be very complicated, even without the special effects that are often needed. The major technique is to consider each part of the scene separately, and then to cover the moves between the various sections. In the simple example above, notice the similarity with the discussion set previously discussed.

It can easily be seen that what takes place in the studio and the lighting arrangement are interdependent. An unforeseen shadow can be very distracting on the screen, and the process of moving the lights so as to eliminate it can waste much valuable studio time. Hence the design of the lighting arrangement to be used should be considered a vital part of the pre-studio programme planning, and the lighting engineer should take part in this planning. The producer can make the lighting engineer's work more easy in the following ways:

1. By allowing sufficient distance between the studio action and the background. Setting the action well forward allows the lighting engineer to light the background separately, and thus to control its level precisely. It also permits the installation of 'back' lights to improve the picture, and keeps distracting shadows off the background.
2. By avoiding the use of shiny, 'brilliant' surfaces. These can produce distracting reflections, which, if sufficiently intense, can even damage the camera tube. Polished surfaces can be suitably dulled by using a special spray, called 'anti-flare', or, more mundanely, by smearing on a *thin* film of soap.

Television in daylight

As we have seen, daylight has two major components – direct light from the sun, and reflected light from the sky. Depending on the weather and the time of day, the proportions of these vary. The direct light from the sun is a hard light giving well defined shadows, and that

166

from the sky is a soft light, filling the shadows, and giving no defined shadows of its own.

Thus, the light from the sun and the light from the sky may be used as key light and filler. However, we cannot move them as we wish to give the modelling we require – we must either move the subject(s) and the camera(s) or wait for the appropriate time of day.

One problem in television is that the sky can be too bright. When it appears in shot, there is high contrast between it and the objects being shown. The television receiver accentuates this difference, whether you are using television cameras or filming and showing the result on telecine, and important teaching points can be lost, even when they are seen clearly on your cine screen or even on the control room monitors.

This effect is stronger when you are shooting towards the sun, so you should avoid doing this if possible, unless you *want* a silhouette effect. If you are filming in black and white, coloured filters (yellow, green, or red) can be used to darken the image of the sky, and with colour film polarising filters can sometimes be used, though this is a difficult technique.

In your planning remember that the sun moves during the day! For a television programme this means estimating where the sun will be during the recording, and for filming it means care with continuity, lest a shadow suddenly jump in the edited sequence.

Where daylight is inadequate, *portable lighting units* can be used. Tungsten halogen (sometimes called quartz iodine) units are convenient and small enough to be carried from place to place. They may be mounted on lightweight stands. Because they are small, however, they produce a hard light – it is inconvenient to carry around the large lamps needed to produce a soft light. You can simply light the whole scene with hard light, accepting the fact that unnatural double shadows will appear in places, but an elegant solution is to use large sheets of white plastic. These reflect the hard lights used for key and background lighting, and because of their size they produce a soft light. They are light-weight, and can even be rolled up into a small space for transport. Some are supplied in the form of an 'umbrella' which can be fixed to a small lamp to reflect a soft light. In black and white work it is often possible to use the ambient daylight or artificial light as a filler to the artificial light that you have installed. In colour work, differences in colour between various light sources are better avoided, and you should block out any other light than the type you are using to light the scene.

Because of the high powers needed, it is generally more convenient for the lights to be powered by mains electricity, but if this is impossible, battery powered units may be used.

11 Appendix III

Designing a floor plan

First, make a rough sketch of the plan that you will need. As an example, we will take a simple case of a programme consisting of a small demonstration by the presenter, preceded and concluded by captions.

First, we need the presenter with his demonstration.

This is the same arrangement described on pages 163–167 and we can add the two cameras.

The bases of the two cameras are shown as circles, with arrows indicating which way they are facing. The angle of view covered by each camera is also marked.

Now we can add the lights, and a cyclorama.

This is the arrangement that we shall try to fit into the studio.

In the studio we are going to use, as in many studios, the cyclorama rail is fixed, so we draw in the cyclorama first. The minimum distance for the back light is determined by the height of the lighting grid, as the spotlamps have no pantographs. The height of the grid is one metre above head level, so the presenter can be three times that distance from the back light – three metres. We can put the back light at the corner of the cyclorama, and the presenter three metres forward from this.

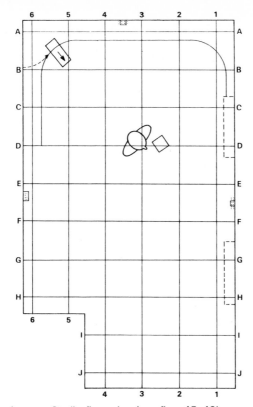

Studio floor plan (see figs. 45–49).

The outline of the lamp used for the back light is the symbol used at this studio for a spot lamp, and its size is not important. The outline of the presenter should however be drawn to scale – most people are about 50cm across – half a metre. The block on which the demonstration stands is also 50cm across.

Now camera 1 faces the presenter. The limitations on the distance between camera and presenter are the following:

1. The camera should not be closer to the demonstration than the minimum focusing distance of its lens – in this case one metre. The angle of the lens must cover the presenter and the demonstration – for a zoom lens we can choose any angle in its range, for a turret we should choose one of the angles that are offered. In this small studio, narrow angles may result in the camera having to be further away than the walls allow. Angles greater than about 35° may give a

169

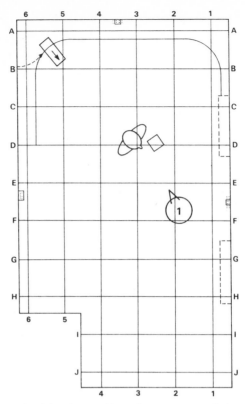

Studio floor plan (showing position of one camera relative to presenter.

somewhat distorted effect. The easiest way is to move a camera angle protractor about on the floor plan until a suitable looking combination of angle and distance is discovered. In this case 35° was found to be convenient.

Camera 2 faces the demonstration. It must stand outside the field of view of camera one, and be beyond the minimum focusing distance. In this case an agle of 16° was used.

The key light should be twice as far away from the presenter as the head to lamp height – so it should be two metres away – and one such distance to one side of the camera-presenter axis, on the side of the demonstration.

The position of the filler is not critical, but should be on the other side of camera one.

The background must also be lit – make sure that you know where

170

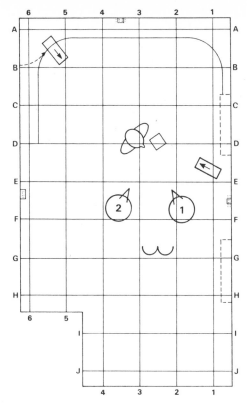

Studio floor plan, showing both cameras and key light.

the background to each shot is. The temptation here is to light the area between A4 and A2, whereas in fact the background to camera 1's shot is B6 to A3 and the background to camera 2's shot is A2 to just past B1.

Now we must find a convenient place for the captions for camera 1 and camera 2. Ideally, they should be able to reach the caption stands with a simple pan, and should be beyond the minimum focusing distance. Again, they have to be lit.

Finally, we add such things as microphones and monitors, and the floor plan is complete.

The numbers and letters at the edges of the plan are repeated on the walls of the studio, and enable any position to be described quickly. By using them, the engineers and the production staff can be sure that their installation exactly matches the floor plan.

171

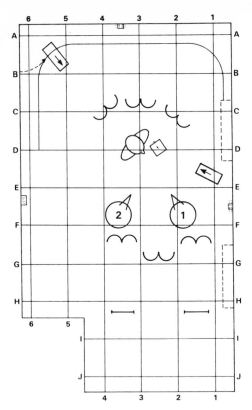

Studio floor plan, showing background lighting.

Camera positions and lens angles

While planning your floor plan, measure the angles that you are expecting your cameras to cover at each stage. You should know what angles are available – either the separate values if your cameras have lens turrets, or the available range if they are fitted with zooms. For most work plan to use fairly wide angles – say in the range 40–25 degrees. Wider angles than this are not usually available; they can be useful in very tight areas, but the result often looks distorted, the perspective apparently being exaggerated, particularly on faces. Narrow angles are useful where cameras run the risk of appearing in each other's shot. Do not use them when you wish to give the impression of depth in a scene, and do not use them if the camera has to move during the shot.

172

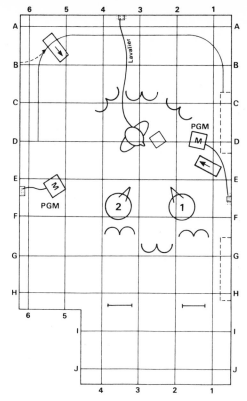

Complete studio floor plan.

Notes on floor plans: camera positions

Mark all positions of cameras – do not leave any out as 'unimportant', or you may come to rehearse and find something large and immovable has been put there!

Mark the first position of camera one as 1A, the second as 1B, and so on.

If a move from one position to the next is to be done in shot, mark it

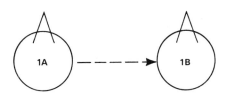

Monitors

Put monitors where they can easily be seen by the people who need to see them.

A person who is going to change captions on a caption stand will find a monitor useful, and for the operator of an animated caption, one is almost indispensable.

An experienced presenter will find one useful, particularly if he has to do a demonstration. Put it in line with his view of the demonstration – this generally means, on the floor.

In this way the presenter can look at the monitor while giving the impression to the viewer that he is looking at the demonstration.

Monitors can also be used by cameramen – for example, see page 129.

12 Appendix IV

Simple film sequences for ETV: the images required

There is a fundamental difference between the way a sequence is made using television equipment and the way it is usually made with film equipment. Whereas making a television sequence is usually a continuous process, filming is almost always done *discontinuously*.

A television sequence is made with a number of television cameras simultaneously viewing the action. The cameras are selected in turn to take their shots, while the action proceeds. In certain special cases – those when an important action cannot possibly be repeated – several film cameras are used simultaneously to make a film sequence. However, it is far more usual to make films by using just one camera. The camera and the action are stopped at the end of filming each shot, and the next shot (which may or may not be the next chronologically in the final film) is then prepared for filming.

This process enables a degree of care and attention to detail in the preparation of each shot which is not always possible in the television studio, where each shot may have to be compromised for the sake of the proceeding and following ones. However, it does allow a type of error that is intrinsically impossible in a continuous recording.

The scene may change between a shot and the one that follows it on the screen in the edited sequence. This is called an error in continuity or a jump cut.

For example, we might film a discussion between two people, first in two shot;

and then in close up

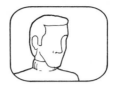

One actor has removed his hat between the taking of one shot and the next, and the result is confusing and distracting. Any number of examples could be given of mysterious changes that have occurred between one shot and the next in filming.

In the professional film industry it is found worthwhile to employ a full time 'continuity girl' to control this problem. She notes every detail of each scene and ensures that all relevant details are 'carried over' from one shot to the next (which may not even be filmed on the same day, or, in a complex production, in the same place!) It is a problem that needs careful attention by every film maker.

Another type of continuity error occurs when the camera is stopped temporarily during a shot. To take an example, a car drives up to some gates in a crowded street, the gates open, and the car drives in. While filming this shot, there is a delay in opening the gates, and the cameraman stops the camera (or, with a spring driven camera, it stops by itself!). The camera is started again as the gates open. There may, or may not, be a 'jump' in the movement of the gates when the result is shown on the screen, but there is certainly a jump in the movement of the pedestrians around the car – indeed some may suddenly vanish!

A solution might be to retake the shot, though we might find that the action was still over-long.

Another solution is to take another shot that can later be shown between the two halves of the main shot.

We might film a close-up of the driver waiting for the gates to open. This shot can be edited between the two parts of the main shot, and there is then no longer a distracting 'jump' on the screen.

This additional shot is called a 'cut-away'.

Notice,that, apart from solving the problem of the error in continuity, the cut-away has also allowed a change in the duration of the scene. The total screen time of the three shots on the screen may well

176

be less than the total time originally taken up by the action. This effect is very useful where a long process must be shown. For example, as part of a process in making a metal box, we wish to show the metal being cut with a flame cutter. Pedagogically, the time taken in cutting is of no intrinsic interest, and the beginning and end of the action will suffice. Yet we do not wish the cutter to 'jump' across the screen. A suitable sequence might be as follows:

MS operator with flame cutter.

CU cutter completing cut.

CU flame cutter starting cut.

MS operator removing tool.

BCU operator's face.

Transitions

Dissolves and split screen effects are available for film work, but require fairly complicated laboratory preparation. For simple sequences it is likely that you will be restricted to straightforward cutting, though you will be able to dissolve to and from the television sequences in the assembly stage.

Pans, zooms, and camera movements can provide effective transitions from shot to shot, but can also make bewildering or distracting changes for the viewer. A pan or a zoom produces an effect of anticipation in the viewer, so if it does not finish on a point of interest it can produce a feeling of frustration.

Thus a useful set of rules is:

1. A pan or a zoom should start at one point of interest and finish on another, unless
2. It is to follow action (in which case, of course, it is continuously on a point of interest).

What is to be avoided in an educational context is a collection of wild swings of the camera that tell more about the director's character than about what is to be taught.

Filming on location

Shooting film away from one's own studios and offices is known as shooting 'on location'. A flowchart follows for filming simple sequences on location, and the following notes refer to this chart.

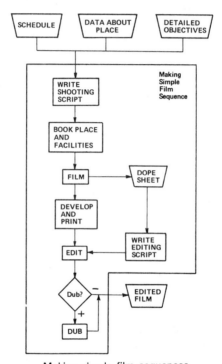

Making simple film sequences.

Shooting script

This is a list of the shots you are intending to take, together with notes, if necessary of how you are going to take them (see example on page 180).

To plan this, you can apply the FASTDOTS rules again. Remember that your audience do not necessarily know the place you are filming or the size and location of the parts you are going to show. Remember that they probably have never been to the place, though you have! Establishing shots, therefore, are usually of great importance, as are the close-ups to meet the fine detail and third dimension requirements.

You may well need to change the duration of operations that you are showing. Remember how cutaways can be used for this purpose. In any case a good selection of potential cutaways will make editing very much easier.

1. MS   Work area – man at cutter
2. 2–S   Man and cutter – lights cutter
3. CU   Sheet put in place
4. CU   Man's face
5. CU   Cutter on sheet
6. CU   Face
7. CU   Cutter on sheet, completes action
8. BCU   Removal of cut item

CHECK LIST WHEN LEAVING FOR LOCATION FILMING
Camera – take up spool
Film
Lenses
Filters
Close-up lenses
Tripod
Pan/tilt head
Exposure meter
Lights
Cables
Plugs/transformers
Reflectors
Anti-flare
Clapper board
Chalk, eraser
Measuring tape
Masking tape
Script
Dope sheets
Blank paper
Pen – flo-pen
Food for crew
Petty cash.

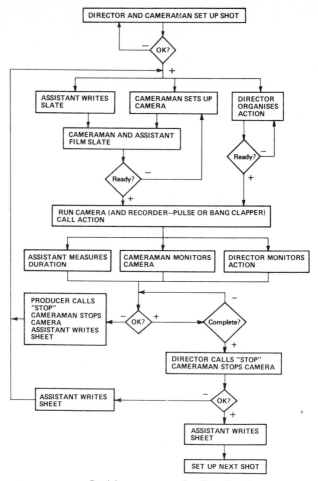

Decision sequence for film direction.

Slate

Careful and consistent use of an identification or board, or 'slate', although apparently time-consuming on location, can make the filming a far more systematic process, and makes the editing of the final result much more straightforward.

Although most people are familiar with the large, black and white striped board seen in large film studios, a small, say 8 x 6in (20cm x 15cm) board is quite adequate for most simple filming. Any carpenter can make one up quickly, and paint it with a surface that will accept chalk. Alternatively, small blackboards can be bought in toyshops. The hinged 'clapper' is not needed for mute filming.

It is useful to put the following information on the board:

180

The code number of the programme
The number of the film roll being used (e.g. roll 1, roll 2, etc)
The number of the shot being filmed
The take number – the first time the shot is attempted the number 1 is added, the second time, number 2 and so on.

These numbers are also written down on an information sheet (dope sheet) by the assistant, together with the duration and details of whether or not the shot was considered successful by the director. Normally the details of the shot as intended are given by the script, and are thus not needed on the dope sheet.

Shots that are added during the film may be given new shot numbers. If the shot was taken so quickly that there was no time to have the slate filmed before it, it may be filmed after the shot, but *upside down*. This prevents confusion with the *following* shot.

Shooting report (dope sheet)

Roll 1. Ident: Prog NS33 seq. 2

1A	25″	Shadow moves across background
1B	30″	OK
2A	10″	Lighter failed
2B	15″	OK
9A	15″	BCU lighter
10A	15″	BCU valve and meter
3A	25″	OK
5A	32″	OK – no board – film ran out

Roll 2. Ident NS33/2 roll 2

5B	30″	OK
7A	30″	OK
8A	15″	Hesitation on action
8B	20″	OK
10A	25″	New shot – BCU cut item

Roll 3. Ident. NS33/3 roll 3.

| 4A | 15″ | OK |
| 6A | 15″ | OK |

News cameramen

Unless your ETV unit is a very large one, with its own film cameramen, you will probably have to work with the cameramen from a commercial television organisation, and this usually implies the use of news cameramen.

News cameramen have their own highly developed skills. They must be able to move into action very quickly at short notice. They must also be able to cover a situation that is 'breaking' very rapidly and possibly unpredictably. Rarely, if ever, is there opportunity for retakes. The need for extreme speed means that they must be able to take shots on their own initiative, in a way that can be edited into a coherent whole. In emergency the film may be put on air with no editing at all.

These characteristics are not those of educational television, with its emphasis on careful, methodical preparation and precision in its execution. If you are going to use a news cameraman, you must remember these differences, and be ready to explain the way of working to the cameraman.

Administration of the site

You will create a lot of disturbance by your operation, whether you are filming or using television cameras. Spectators will almost certainly gather, and there will be people who want to know what is going on. As director, your priority is to get the best possible pictures (and sound). It may not be a good idea to break your concentration and that of your team to deal with visitors.

It is a good idea to have an assistant who can concern himself exclusively with the administration of the area. He should be able to distinguish between those who have a right to be in the area and those who should be discouraged. He should know enough about the operation to be able to explain it to important people who suddenly arrive. He should have sufficient diplomatic skill to dissuade such people from interfering with the filming. He may find it useful to put up a rope to separate 'spectators' from 'workers', and in the case of work with television cameras he may find it useful to have a monitor that spectators can see. He should have a good idea of how much time the operation is going to take, and how the various parts are to be split up. If, on top of all this, he can produce coffee at the right moment, he will be loved by all!

The most frequently asked question on location is 'When can we see the result?' If you know the date of transmission, have it put on the script, and make sure that your administrative assistant knows it.

He can put it up on a large blackboard to avoid being asked the same question too many times!

It is a good safeguard to obtain written permission from each of the participants for the use of the film or the recording. The assistant may have a stack of 'waiver forms' which specifically waive any copyright the participant may have in the result, and get them signed. Whatever the legal necessity, this certainly avoids your being pestered for special payments long after the transmission is over.

Filming in a studio

As filming is normally done with just one camera, with stops between shots, a film studio does not have the complicated control arrangements of a television studio. The director spends most of his time near the film cameraman (in a big studio he sits on the camera crane) where he can see what is going on. The difficulties of doing this have led some studios to install TV cameras in the film camera viewfinders, and some have even installed multiple cameras with TV facilities and the operation is run like a television studio.

Lighting facilities are similar to those in a television studio, with the advantage that adjustments can be made for individual shots, something normally impracticable in a television studio.

Processing

After filming, the film is delivered to the processing laboratory with the following information: The number of rolls and their production identity, the film speed rating on which the exposure was based. Whether the film should be processed as 'reversal' – giving a positive result only – or as 'neg/pos' giving a negative and a positive.

While the film is being processed, you can use the shooting report to write an editing script. This is a list, in order, of the shots you intend to put together to make the sequence you need.

Separating shots

A large film studio, working with 35mm or larger film, only prints the shots marked on the dope sheet as being successful. However, in 16mm work it is usual for the director to receive a positive copy of all that he has shot.

First you must know if you are going to use the actual positive copy you have received as your copy (after editing) for telecine. If you are, you must take all the necessary precautions to see that the film is not damaged in any way, because any damage will be seen when the film is shown on telecine. You will have to handle the film only by its edges, and/or wear light linen gloves while editing. You can forget those precautions if the edited film is going to be used only as a guide for an editor to cut the negative and make a new positive copy from that.

Run the film through once, on a projector or on a high quality viewer, to check that your comments on the shooting report – and thus your editing script – are correct. If there is any discrepancy, this is a good moment to revise your editing script.

Now use a viewer, identify each of the boards in turn and cut the film into each of its constituent shots. Hang the sections of the film up, on the editing rack, or, if one is not available, by pieces of sticky tape on a window or a wall.

Now use the editing script to assemble the shots you have chosen, in order.

View the result, preferably on a motorised viewer. It may, if you are lucky, be quite satisfactory as it is. More likely, you will find that some at least of the shots are too long, or contain unnecessary information. Use a wax pencil to mark 'better' beginning and end points for each shot, and then cut and rejoin the film using these marks.

When the film looks quite satisfactory on the viewer, take it and view it on a film projector. Flaws may show up with the better picture quality that were not visible when the film went through the viewer. Edit again, and repeat the process until the sequence is satisfactory.

If serious problems arise, you may have to change the shot order and/or reselect shots from the pegboard. Notice that this simple technique only allows the straight cut as a transition from one shot to another. You can however, dissolve, wipe, and so on, to and from the preceding or following sequence in the studio. You can also superimpose a graphic that is in the studio. For that matter, using the studio vision mixer, you can fade to and from black.

If you are intending to add a commentary, this is a good time to write it, as you can check the result by reading it aloud while running the film.

As always in ETV, the sound should complement the picture, and not compete with, duplicate, or dominate it. A film commentary should meet these requirements. As we noted in the case of graphics (see page 111), the video makes a concept specific, and so the audio can make general statements that cannot be made by the video. However, if you have made the film well, you will probably find that few words are necessary. Certainly you can avoid describing what the viewer can perfectly well see for himself. If you find the words 'as you can see' in the commentary, this is a good indication that the commentary is superfluous, at least at this point. Occasionally it is useful to prewarn the viewer of what is going to happen 'Now watch what happens when the black bird tries to join the flock. . . .' 'Watch how his body turns as he kicks. . . .'

Generally, however, the fewer words the better.

Well chosen sound effects can help establish the atmosphere of the scene.

There are four ways of adding sound to a film sequence for television.

1. Use the film, in telecine, as a source of picture only, adding sound from the studio.
2. Add a magnetic stripe to the film and record on that, using a projector with magnetic recording capability. To use this, telecine must have magnetic stripe playback facilities.
3. Record on a separate magnetic film, using either a double band project or a recorder interlocked with the projector. Again telecine must have compatible playback facilities.
4. Record onto VTR, using telecine, recording sound either simultaneously or later ('audio dub').

Of these, the first is perhaps the most usual; the advantage of the other methods, apart from allowing the commentary to be recorded at leisure, is that they free the studio for elaborate (and noisy) resetting.

Methods involving optical sound are of course available, but are suitable and economic only for large quantities of copies.

Do not expect to be able to record on an ordinary audio tape recorder and maintain synchronism with the projector and/or telecine. The sound and picture are bound to get out of step at some point, probably during recording of the programme!

If you need to record complex and/or accurately synchronised sound effects, the best place to do this is a film dubbing theatre, with its expert crew.

Finally, add opening and closing leaders as required by the telecine unit. Measure the duration of the sequence(s) either by means of a stopwatch or by putting the film through a film measurer.

Bibliography

A study of Thinking, Bruner, J., Goodnow, J. J., and Austin, G. A., New York Science Editors 1967.

Educational Psychology: A Cognitive View, Auswbel, D. P., Holt, Rinehart, and Winston, New York 1968.

Principles of Instructional Design, Gagne, R. M., and Briggs, C. J., Holt, Rinehart, and Winston, New York 1968.

Script Continuity and the Production Secretary, Rowlands, A., Focal Press, London 1977.

The Technique of Documentary Film Production, Baddeley, H., Focal Press, London 1975.

The Technique of Editing 16mm Films, Burder, J., Focal Press, London 1971.

The Technique of Television Production, Millerson, G., Focal Press, London 1972.

TV Lighting Methods, Millerson, G., Focal Press, London 1975.

Glossary

Accountability   Evaluation of an educational system as a whole.

Animated film   Film made by stop motion. (See *Focal Encyclopedia of Film and Television Techniques*, p. 783.)

Animated Graphic   A caption with movement produced by moving parts of the graphic.

Anti-flare   Aerosol spray used to reduce reflections from shiny surfaces. Also called Dulling spray.

Assistant director   A person to whom part of the director's responsibilities are delegated.

Audio   Signal containing information which can be decoded to give programme sound.

Back light   Light directed towards the camera from behind the subject. Also called "rim light".

Behavioural objective   An objective that describes the observable behaviour or ability of the viewer after watching the programme.

Camera card   Card attached to camera giving information about planned shots.

Camera tube   The unit which converts the pattern of light formed by the lens into electrical impulses (the video signal). Colour cameras may have three or four.

Channel   Pair of frequencies on which a TV programme is transmitted.

Character generator   Electronic unit which can put words on the TV screen without using a camera.

Clapper   Hinged board on slate which can be used in sound filming to give sync information.

Close-up (1) Of person: shot showing head and shoulders.
(2) Of object: shot showing object large in frame.

Closed circuit TV System on which all signals are passed by cable.

Closed reception Reception in which the audience and the utilization are controlled.

Content objectives An objective that describes what is to be taught by a programme.

Continuity Illusion of continuous action maintained through a sequence of shots which may not have been filmed at the same time.

Cover shot Shot showing complete area of action.

Credits Word captions giving information about the programme.

Criteria – referenced testing Testing to establish how far objectives were achieved.

Critical assessment Testing a programme by having it viewed by a group of experts.

Cueing Giving a signal to a participant in a programme, e.g. to a presenter to start speaking.

Diffusor Frame with layer of material fitted in front of lamps to soften the light.

DIN print One of the possible arrangements of emulsion, sprocket holes, and picture on a film print.

Director's assistant Person responsible for calling shots, giving telecine timings, etc.

Editing rack A bar with pins on which lengths of film are hung.

Emergency direction Method of direction based on explaining shots to cameramen while the programme is in progress.

ENG Electronic News Gathering. Method of obtaining news material by using hand held camera and a portable recorder (videotape or videocassette).

EPF Electronic Production in the Field. Attempts to apply the techniques of ENG to making planned programmes.

Essential area The part of the television picture area which can safely (?) be used for teaching information.

Evaluation Measurements of inputs, process, and outputs, used to improve the system.

Evaluation contract An agreement between producer and evaluator as to what will be the objectives of a programme and what amount of change is to be expected in the viewers.

Experimental objectives An objective that describes the experience that will be given to the viewer by the programme.

Fastdots A mnemonic used in this book for the limitations of a television picture – see page 136.

Feedback Information given to a system about its output.

Fill light/filler Soft light used to reduce density of shadows.

Floor plan Plan of shooting area used to plan positioning of technical equipment, setting and programme action.

Fold back Loudspeakers connected to all programme sound except microphones.

Format Outline of programme content.

Front axial projection Equipment using projector mounted on camera with mirror and reflecting screens to show slides or films as part of television picture.

Graphics Drawn or photographed material for a television programme.

Hard light Light that produces dense, well defined shadows.

Headset Earphones used by cameramen and other personnel for communication, sometimes with microphone.

Insert (1) Sequence on film or videotape used as part of programme.

        (2) Method of editing videotape by using a control track which is kept unchanged when sequences or parts of sequences are replaced.

Instructional objectives See Objective.

Jig-saw assembly Videotape editing together of sequences not necessarily in the order in which they were recorded.

Key light Light used to produce modelling effect on subject.

Library film Film already prepared and used before production of the programme.

Line up Period for adjustment before recording or transmission.

Long cable techniques Use of cameras and microphones outside the studio while still connected to the studio systems.

Media combination The various media used together in a teaching situation.

Microphone boom Controllable unit for suspending microphone near programme participants without appearing in shot.

Mobile unit Vehicle with control room for use with cameras and microphones. Generally contains videorecording equipment.

Modelling Arrangement of light and shadow to give illusion of third dimension in TV picture.

Monitor (1) Unit with video signal as input and picture as output.
(2) Supervisor in television classroom.
Multiburst Video signal containing set of frequencies, used for checking equipment.

Narrow angle lens Lens with acceptance angle of 20° or less.
Norm-referenced testing Testing that results in a list of students in order of acquired ability.

O.B. – outside broadcast Sequence(s) made by mobile unit (q.v.).
O.B. – outside broadcast A vehicle with cameras and control room for producing programmes or sequences away from the studio.
Objective A description of the aim or purpose of a programme – see Behavioural objective, Content objective, Experiential objective, Process objective.
Open reception Reception in which the audience is not prescribed or directly controlled.

Pan Horizontal rotation of camera.
Polarising filter Filter used for reducing the effect of reflections and for darkening skies on colour film.
Process objectives An objective that describes the mental process expected of the students.

Quartz iodine Small, high intensity lamp used for filming. Also called tungsten halide.

Receiver (TV) Equipment that has radio frequency (from an aerial) as input, picture and sound as output.
Reliability (of evaluation) Whether tests measure accurately and consistently.
Reverse modelling Unnatural effect produced when fill light is stronger than key light.
Run through A rehearsal of the programme in which the whole programe is attempted without stopping.

Safe area See Essential area.
Signal Electrical wave form containing information.
Signal (1) Video signal. The set of electrical impulses that can be fed to a monitor to produce a picture.
(2) Audio signal. The electrical voltages that can be fed to an amplifier and loudspeaker to produce sound.
Single frame image Image without movement produced by *some* videotape or videocassette machines when the tape is stopped.

SMPTE print An alternative to the DIN print (q.v.) with different geometry.

Soft light Light that produces faint, ill-defined shadows, if any.

Stagger through Rehearsal with frequent stops to correct errors.

Standby Period between lineup and transmission or recording.

Subsystem If the process and inputs of system B are part of the process of system A, then system B is a subsystem of process A.

Superimposition Combination of two TV pictures by simple addition of the two signals.

Suprasystem If system B is a subsystem of system A, then system A is a suprasystem of system B.

Sync sound Sound that is synchronised with movement in picture.

Synthetics Images produced without use of camera.

System There are two definitions: (1) A set of interrelated parts. (2) Something that produces a change.

All the systems in this book fit *both* definitions.

Systematic direction Method of direction in which pre-prepared shot numbers, camera cards, and scripts replace direct orders from the director.

Talk back Communication system between personnel in the control room and those on studio floor (or action area).

Telecine Unit which has slides and/or motion picture film as input, video and/or audio signals as output.

Teleprompter Equipment for showing scripts to presenter while he is looking at the camera lens.

Ten light Unit with ten light sources to produce soft light.

Test card Pattern used for adjusting cameras and other equipment.

Tilt Movement of camera, rotating about horizontal axis at right angles to lens axis.

Track configuration Arrangement of tracks on tape. This is an important factor when using audio or video recordings on different machines.

Tungsten halide See Quartz iodine.

Turret camera Camera with several lenses mounted on rotating plate.

Two-shot Shot with two subjects.

Validity Whether tests actually measure what they are intended to measure.

Video Signal which can be used as input to monitor to give picture as output.

Videocassette Container for videotape permitting rapid loading and unloading of records designed to take them.

Videotape Magnetic tape used for recording and reproducing video and audio signals.

Vision mixer (1) Equipment for selecting and combining video signals.
(2) Person who operates this equipment.

VTR (1) Videotape recording.
(2) The equipment for videotape recording.
(3) The personnel who operate this equipment.

Wide angle lens (in TV) Lens with angle of acceptance wider than about 25°.

Wild sound Sound recorded with no attempt to synchronise it with camera.

Zoom Lens with variable angle of acceptance. (Strictly, one that holds focus while varying angle of acceptance.)

Index